TROUT

TROUT

A Fictitious History

DAN BROWN

Granite Creek Press

CONTENTS

Introduction

As far back as I can remember I have been interested in fish. This is not exactly true as my first recollections of animals are of snakes and box elder bugs...well I think they were box elder bugs, but I was only 4 or 5 years old and they may have been a similar looking hemipteran. How does this happen? Why do some people like ducks, or deer, or fast cars, or even adding up numbers in tidy columns? I have my theory.

My love of fish was predetermined by the stars. I was born a Pisces to a fisherman and his wife. The fisherman was not a fisherman by trade, but loved to fish for fun and food. At a young age I started fishing. My first fish of note was a carp from the Sacramento River that was half as long as I was tall. From there I moved to Brown Bullheads in the Pit River of northern California. In northern Idaho, I was introduced to trout fishing. There was a beautiful creek a stone's throw from our side door where I spent most summer mornings catching grasshoppers and the afternoons floating them through pools full of hungry rainbows. A little later, my father and I would fish an impoundment of Lower Crab Creek in Washington State. Here we pulled Muddler Minnows behind plastic bubbles where they were attacked by 18" Rainbows and Browns. In college, which was located in a county with one fishable lake (what was I thinking?), I was introduced to fly fishing with a fly rod by my roommate, Glenn. I bought a fiberglass Fenwick at the Husky gas station in Moscow, Idaho. Glenn taught me how to cast among jeers of "Catching any?" on the intramural sports fields of WSU.

What I like best about fishing can be distilled down to three reasons. Fishing is an acceptable excuse to stop working and be outside. The feel of a fish at the end of my line makes me feel particularly alive, it pulses like a beating heart, causing mine to accelerate. The underwater world is mysterious, we never really know what is down there. Of course, in this modern age, that is not as true, but when I was a kid, it was. You never really know what marvelous fish will surface.

Emily Carr Sculpin

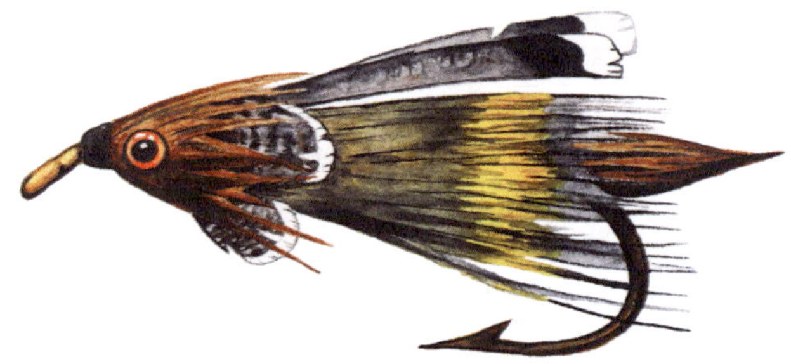

Emily Carr Sculpin
*Materials: Camel hair watercolor brush bristles, Sooty
Grouse Feathers, Black-tailed Deer hair, and artificial sculpin
eyes*

Notes

The inspiration for this book came from a chance encounter with Erik Rockliffe at Boo Radley's Gift Shop in Spokane, Washington. My North 40 fly fishing hat prompted a fishing conversation which included Redbands he caught in the Spokane River. I faked my way through the conversation and when I got home, I Goggled Redbands, as I didn't know what they were. It turns out that I had been catching Redbands off and on throughout my life and I did not even know it. However, in my mind, a band should go around the fish, not along the lateral line. My first painting was of the Columbia River Redband Trout with a big red band around the middle.

I used James Prosek's wonderful "Trout: An Illustrated History" book as a reference for my own artistic version of the other varieties of trout. I painted for three winters, usually at the kitchen table on Saturday and Sunday mornings while I watched birds at the feeder just outside the window. Then I started letting my mind wander and combined facts with my fiction to come up with little histories and explanations for colorings and markings of these made-up trout. The whole process was quite enjoyable. I learned a lot about trout from James Prosek's writings and my own little bit of research.

This book is only possible because James Prosek created the stunningly beautiful and well written book "Trout: An Illustrated History". He created it when he was just a young adult. I am reaching the old man stage. I have used his paintings and writings to inspire my images and writing. I would buy his book as a companion to mine. Heck, I would buy his first any day.

In this book, most of the names are real, but the images have been changed to match how my imagination sees them. Many of the facts are true, but they are mixed in liberally with the fiction. I did research the fish and their new look, so there are bits of reality in the images too. I am not a purist about anything. I fish spoons, flies, and real grasshoppers. I eat Thai and Italian dishes in the same meal. And yes, I use white gouache when I watercolor.

Most of the paintings have been adjusted in Photoshop Elements. I used Arches cold press 140 lb. (300 gsm) watercolor paper stretched wet on an old drawing board. Daniel Smith's watercolors were used for two reasons: they are really good watercolors and are made in my home state. I prefer round watercolor brushes. I would have used Kolinsky sable brushes, if I could have afforded them. They really are the Cadillac of watercolor brushes. Boy, I must be old using Cadillacs as the standard. I wonder what the new automobile standard is? I did use the Subarus of watercolor brushes. (Subarus are very dependable cars for us who live in the snowy North and are reasonably priced.)

CHAPTER 1

CHAR

This group of trout are believed to be named after the French poet René Char. There are two plausible reasons for the selection of his surname for this diverse group of trout. René was a surrealist and indeed the markings on these fish could have been painted by the likes of Salvador Dalí or René Magritte. The other is that René was a fighter, much like these fish, earning the Medal of the Resistance and the Croix de Guerre for fighting with the French Resistance.

https://www.poetryfoundation.org/poets/rene-char

Arctic Char

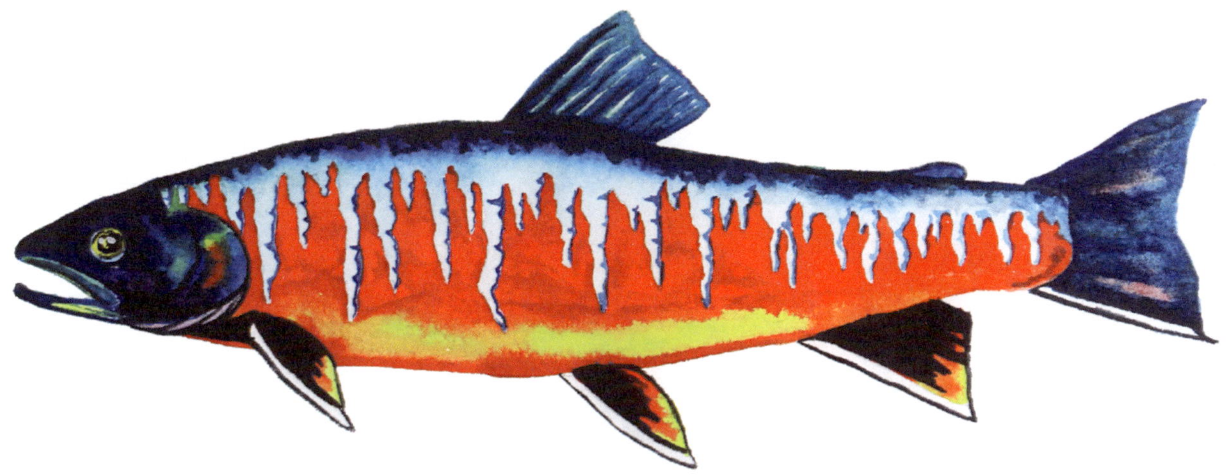

Salvelinus alpinus alpinus

Arctic Char sounds like a burger from the menu of an Arctic Circle restaurant. I did a search and it is not. Arctic Char sounds oxymoronic, like jumbo shrimp. How in the heck can it be Arctic and charred at the same time? It is not as far-fetched as it seems. I recall a winter camping trip my wife and I took on Loup Loup Pass. After dinner we stood around one of the coldest fires I have ever stood around. I swear it was not giving off any heat. If I had not been careful, I could have charred my boots without feeling heat from the fire. The next day when we returned home we found out the temperature had been 5º F. Being a fisherman, I should probably exaggerate and say it was 30º F below zero, as for much of the far North, 5º F is a heat wave. My wife, besides being a great cook and my skate ski partner, is very creative. She gets the credit for the combination of icicles and fire on this char. Some September, I hope to fish for Arctic Char and hunt Caribou with my camera.

https://acburger.com/menu.html

Greenland Char

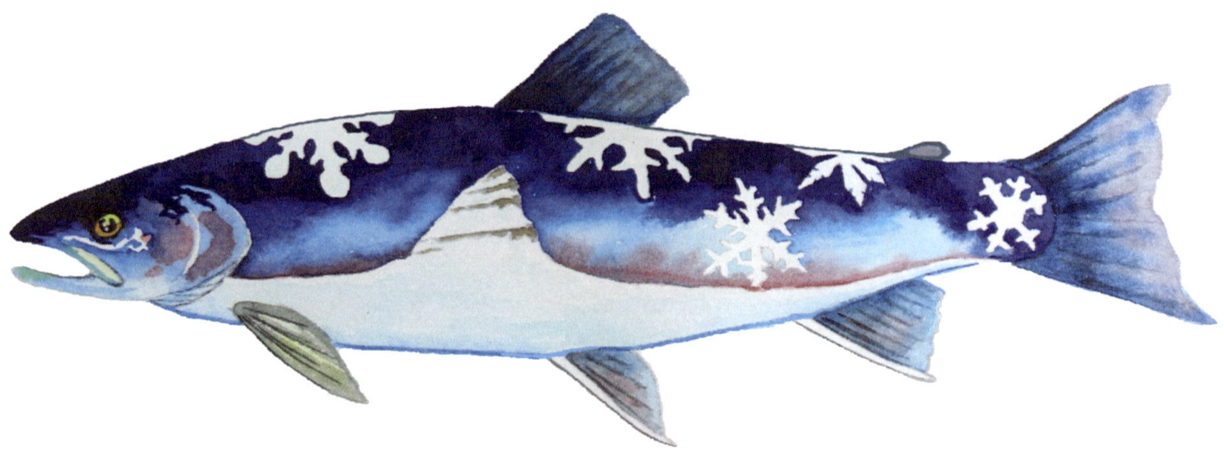

Salvelinus alpinus stagnalis

There is some discussion in ichthyological circles that the Greenland Char should really be called the Icelandic Char. The evidence these ichthyologists use to argue the Icelandic origin are the snowflake patterns on the dorsal surface of this char. While Greenland is the icier of the two countries, the snowflakes and their arrangement seem strangely familiar. Any visit to the duty-free shop at the Keflavik International Airport in Iceland will overwhelm you with snowflakes on the warm and beautiful Icelandic sweaters. In addition, the white triangle on the lateral surfaces resembles Kirkjufell Mountain which is in Iceland. Before you pooh-pooh the idea that fish cannot change to match their surroundings, pay attention to the trout caught in your favorite little creek. I am always amazed at how much they match the creek bottom. Conversely, place a beautiful trout in an aquarium and they bleach out to a barely recognizable fish. This is more of a reach, but the image of Kirkjufell Mountain on the side of the Greenlandic Char looks like a shark dorsal fin. All tourist books of Iceland love to tell us about the fermented shark dish in Iceland. The Greenland Char is a literal swimming billboard for the Icelandic Tourist Board.

https://www.earthtrekkers.com/iceland-bucket-list-best-things-to-do-in-iceland/

Blueback Trout

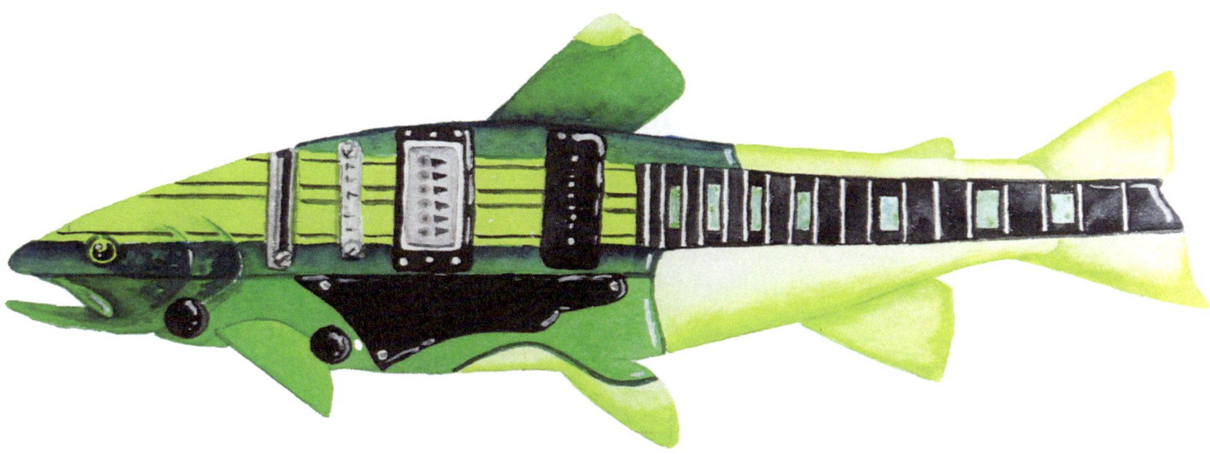

Salvelinus alpinus oquassa

The Blueback Trout is commonly called the Bluesback Trout. It has the ability to change its marking at will, much like squid. Researchers have not found a connection between the markings and physical backgrounds, moods of the fish, reproductive state, or season. It seems this trout loves blues music and changes its markings with some internal blues radio station. In the same river on the same day, even minutes apart, diligent researchers (fishermen) have caught this trout with the markings of BB King's "Lucille", Lightening Hopkin's Gibson J-160E hollow box , and Lead Belly's Stella. The markings quickly fade when removed from the water. The example included here is of the Reverend guitar designed by Blues great Rick Vito. Recently, I listened to Rick playing with Mick Fleetwood's Blues Band at the Fox Theater in Spokane, Washington. Not only is he a superb musician, he has great rapport with the audience. The Fox Theater in Spokane is well worth a visit with its renovated Art Deco décor.

https://www.earlyblues.com/Blues%20Artists%20and%20Their%20Instruments%202012.htm
https://foxtheaterspokane.org/
https://www.rickvito.com/

Baffin Char

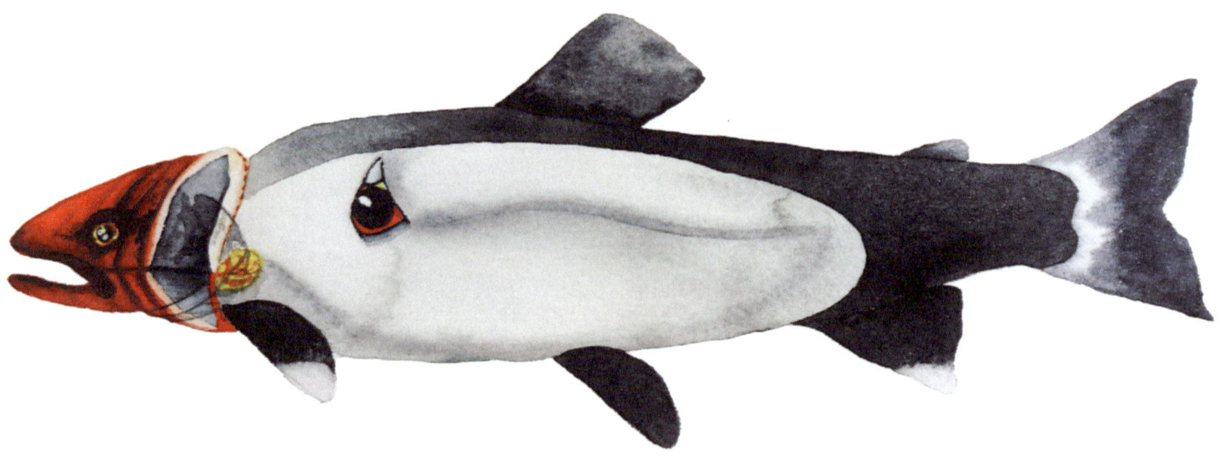

Salvelinus alpinus naresi

Baffin Island is the largest island in Canada and the fifth largest in the world. The Atlantic Puffin frequents its waters and shores. The largest breeding populations of Atlantic Puffin can be found a little further south near Witless Bay, Newfoundland. The Baffin Char has evolved to fool the feeding Atlantic Puffin. Diving puffins are so surprised to be confronted by the head of a giant puffin that they drop their current catch and blast to the surface. It takes them up to an hour to recover from their fright. (Puffins have a cool barbed tongue which allow them to hold their current catch while they catch more before returning to shore to eat or feed their young.) The current use of miniature "Go-Fish" cameras to study the behavior and lives of minnows to Mekong Catfish has greatly advanced fish science. "Go-Fish" cameras on Baffin Char have resulted in hilarious YouTube videos of the surprised looks on attacking Atlantic Puffins' faces. Some days they have had more views than adorable cat videos.

https://en.wikipedia.org/wiki/Baffin_Island

Sunapee Trout

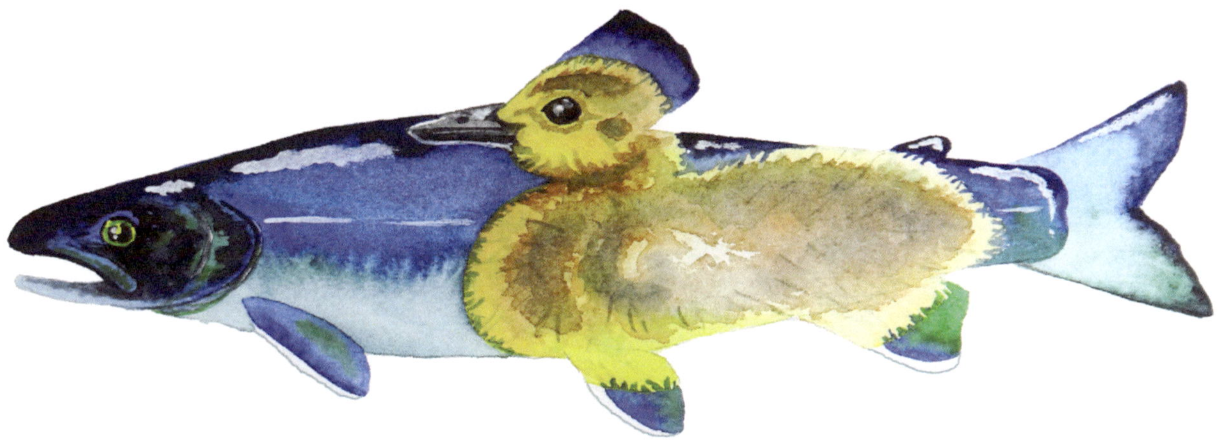

Salvelinus alpinus aureolus

Sunapee is an Algonquin word (Soo-Nipi) meaning Wild Goose Waters because it is a stopping over spot for migrating geese. Interestingly, from the air Lake Sunapee is in the shape of a flying goose. Once the Sunapee Trout was quite small and hardly noticed by fisherman. Over time the almost sterile waters of this glacial lake have become more fertile, partially due to the fertilizing efforts of the geese that use this lake. The Sunapee Trout responded by eating more and growing larger. Once large enough, the Sunapee Trout added goslings to their diet, allowing them to grow even larger. Here lies an amazing physical and behavioral transformation of the Sunapee Trout. Their daffodil yellow spots became fewer and larger until one in the shape of a happy little gosling became the predominant spot. Now a unique hunting method can be observed. Several large trout will spread out in a line. A decoy trout will swim just under the surface to a brood of goslings. This decoy will then erratically swim head down bringing its gosling-shaped spot above the water. Once the goslings start following it, it leads them to the line of hungry diners.

https://en.wikipedia.org/wiki/Lake_Sunapee

Quebec Red Trout

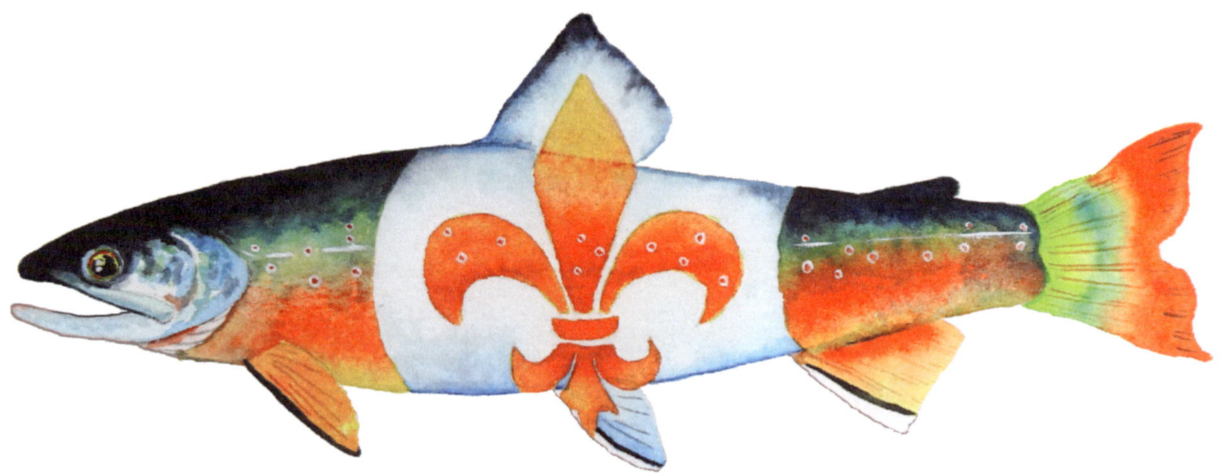

Salvelinus alpinus marstoni

The Quebec Red Trout is very proud of its Canadian homeland and its Quebecois roots. This is evident with the large red fleur-de-lis gracing its sides. There is a provincial myth that the Quebec Red Trout furiously attacks flies made in England and British Columbia. This is only a myth. Researchers have attached an aquatically modified universal testing machine between their casting line and leader and have found out they attack all lures and flies equally, they just happen to be furious fighters. The Quebec Red is favored for its smoking qualities. This trout naturally has a real maple flavor. They are also delicious fried right from the lake with camp pancakes (slightly burnt and often shaped like Mickey Mouse) and cowboy coffee.

https://en.wikipedia.org/wiki/Universal_testing_machine

Lake Hazen Char

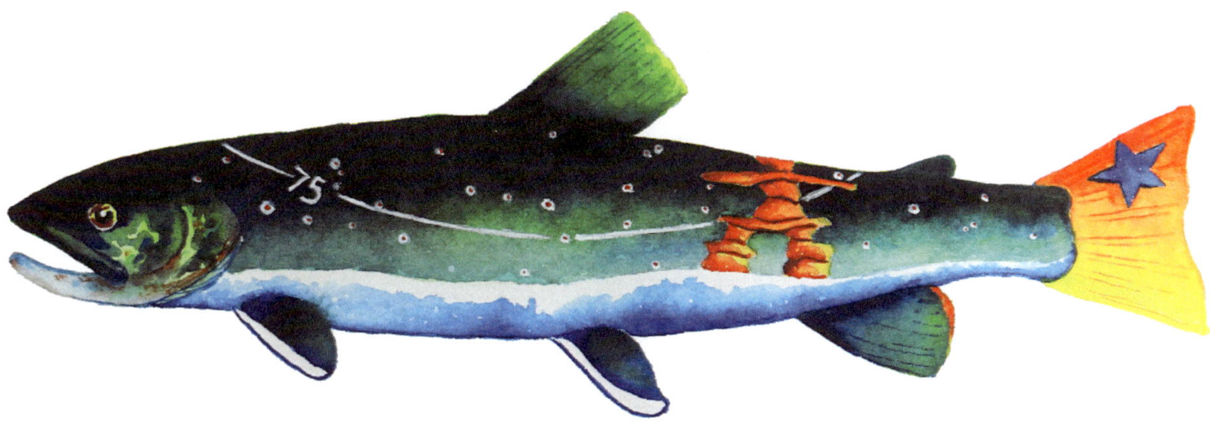

Salvelinus alpinus arcturus

The Lake Hazen Char has the historical distinction of being caught to help supply Admiral Robert Perry and Matthew Henson on their expedition to the North Pole. Lake Hazen is a large lake that lies entirely above the Arctic Circle on Ellesmere Island. While the reaching of the North Pole was an amazing feat, living day to day at high latitudes for millennia is even more amazing. The sides of the Lake Hazen Char honor those who live in this harsh climate. For those of us that live at lower latitudes, it seems impossible that humans and animals can thrive in winters with such extreme cold and long winter nights. The dark sides of the Lake Hazen Char mimic the dark winter night sky with its brilliant constellations. The stacked stone figure and star, the symbols of Canada's Nunavut Territory, also grace its sides.

http://collections.dartmouth.edu/arctica-beta/html/EA15-55.html
http://www.thecanadianencyclopedia.ca/en/article/ellesmere-island/
https://en.wikipedia.org/wiki/Nunavut

Long-Finned Char

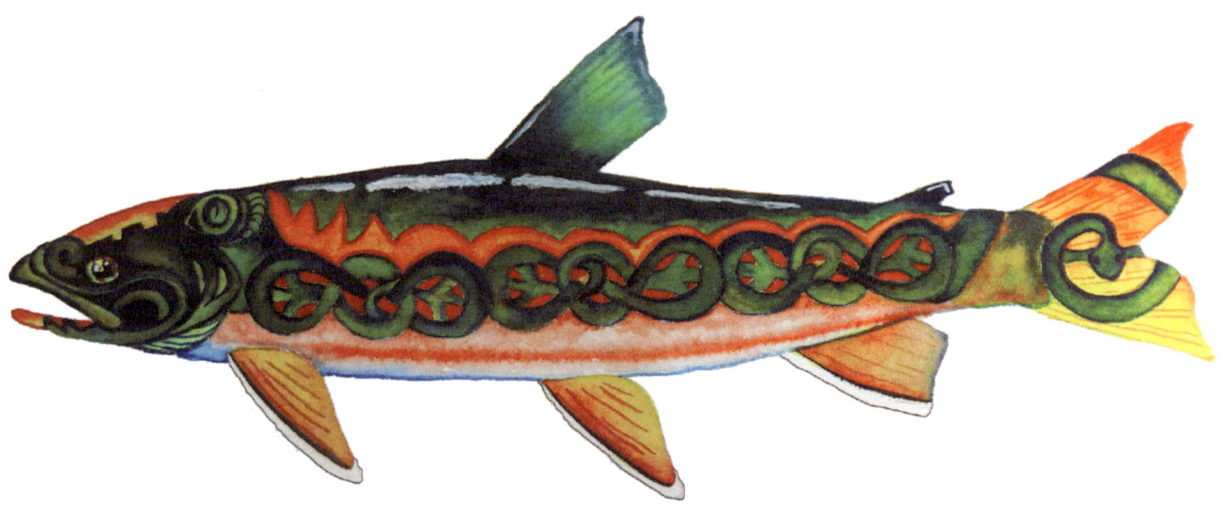

Salvelinus alpinus alipes

The fins on this char are longer than those of any other char. While not as long as those of Flying Fish, they look just as unusual. These char live in Greenland and the Boothia Peninsula of Nunavut, Canada. The longer fins perhaps indicate a Scandinavian origin. The average height of Greenlanders is 1.629 meters for men and 1.538 meters for women and the average height of Swedish males is 1.79 meters and 1.65 meters for women. Some factors in Scandinavia seem to encourage a greater size.

The markings on the sides of the Long-Finned Char also point to a Scandinavian origin. The long green markings are similar to those found on Viking ships. However, the weaving designs also bear resemblance to Celtic designs, Arabic tessellating tiles, and the art of the Dutch artist M. C. Escher, which leaves room for further research and fishing trips.

https://www.jstor.org/stable/660541?seq=1#metadata_info_tab_contents
https://www.insider.com/tallest-people-world-countries-ranked-2019-6#16-sweden-17271cm-5-feet-799-inches-10

Brook Trout

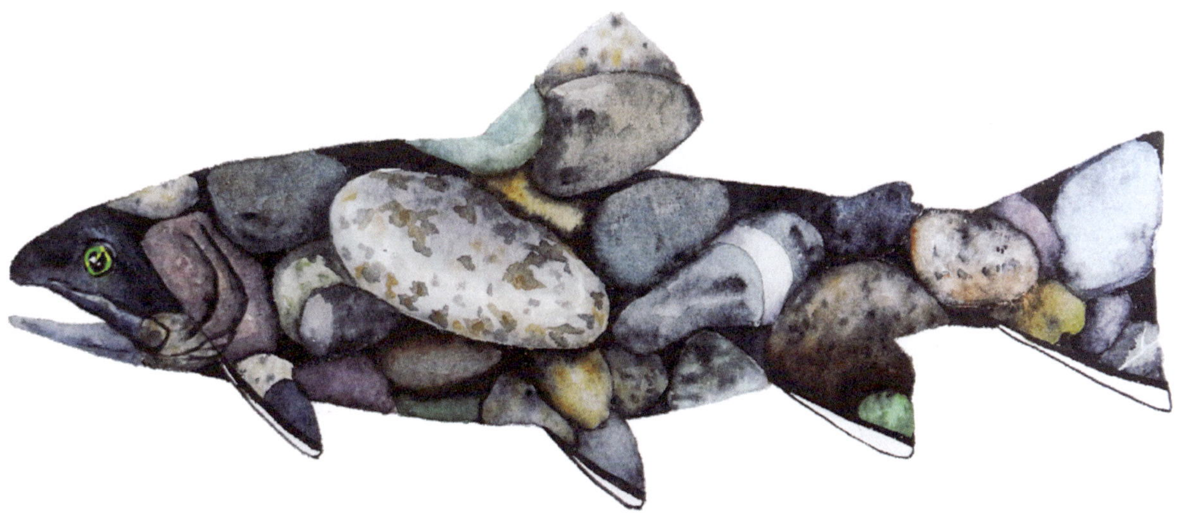

Salvelinus fontinalis fontinalis

Spawning Brook Trout are extremely stunning. Their tigerish belly colors just make me happy. Of course, it is not just coincidence, catching a fish always makes me happy. The special joy of catching a spawning Brookie can be explained by color theory research. Orange is made, in the painting world, from a mixture of red (I prefer Napthol Red) and yellow (Cadmium Yellow Medium). Orange combines the high energy of red and the joy of yellow. It is intensified by being contrasted with black. Orange is believed to increase oxygen to the brain, thus energizing you and helping you think better.

However, orange attracts attention and not just the attention of possible mates. Predators also love spawning season as their prey are easier to spot. Most of the year Brook Trout wear cryptic coloration. They have an uncanny ability to match the substrate of their home body of water. This is one of the fun reasons I enjoy catching Brookies. An empty appearing body of water often magically results in a nice limit of Brookies. Their coloration closely matching their backgrounds results in a stunning variety of camouflage colors and shapes.

Labrador Trout

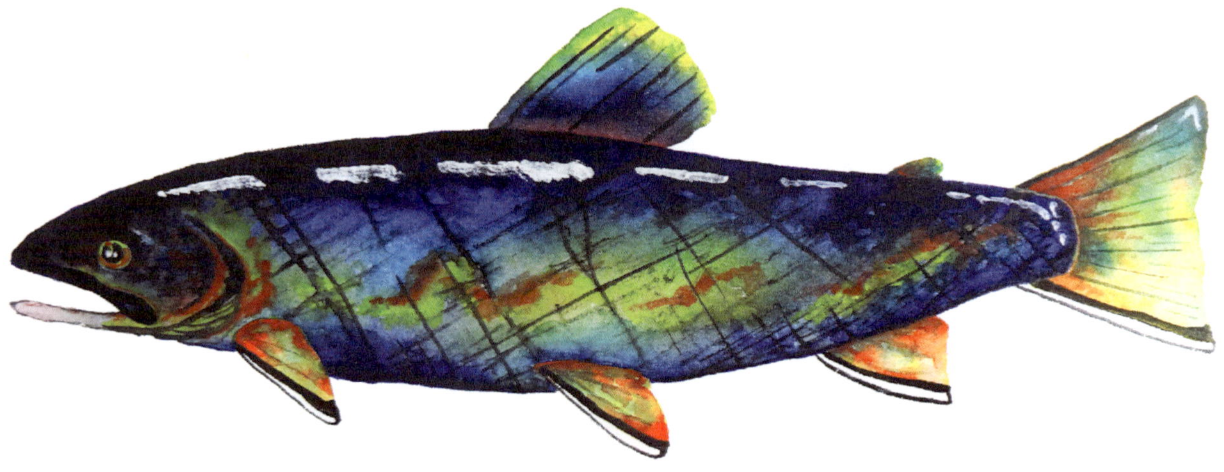

Salvelinus fontinalis fontinalis

The Labrador Trout is another example of how Brook Trout match the stream bottom. This trout matches the colors of Labradorite, a gemstone from the province of Newfoundland and Labrador. The stone was first written about by Moravian missionaries on the Isle of St. Paul. The gemstone and the trout exhibit an iridescence called labradorescence.

On a side note, the people of Labrador and Newfoundland are fearless. My wife and I hiked from Cappahayden to Witless Bay on the East Coast Trail. When it says it follows the East Coast, it means it. Often the trail edges a cliff that plunges to the sea. On this hike, we spent a delightful afternoon with the artist John Chidley and his wife, Rita. We asked him where we could get some water and he took us to his house where he filled our water bottles and cooked us up some delicious cod. We walked past the lighthouse where he grew up. His mother used to carry him, his siblings, and supplies, up an eighty foot rickety ladder, to the lighthouse perched at the edge of the cliff.

https://geology.com/gemstones/labradorite/#:~:text=Labradorite%20is%20a%20feldspar%20mineral,be%20the%20most%20abundant%20mineral

Silver Trout

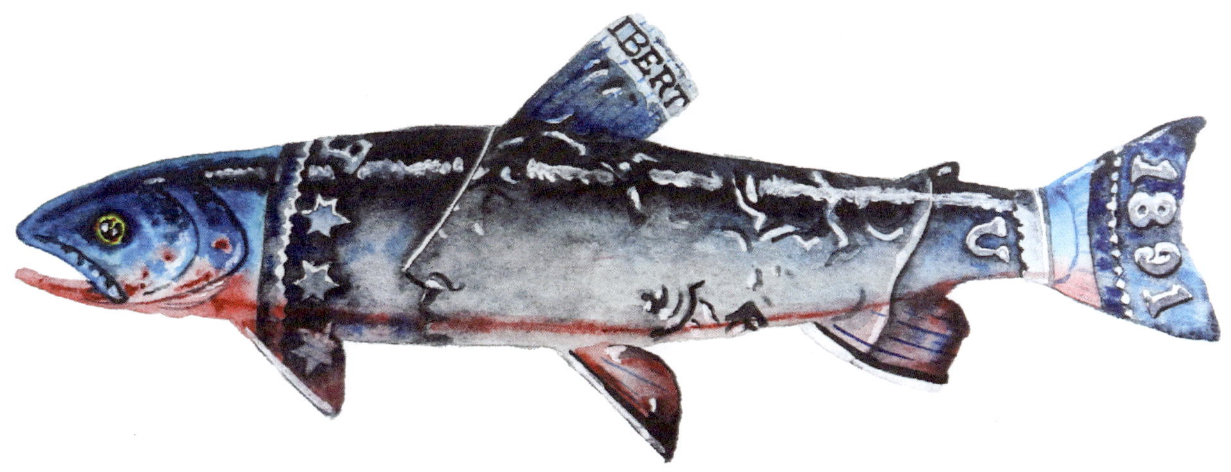

Salvelinus fontinalis agassiz

Sadly, like the minting of the Morgan silver dollar, the Silver Trout no longer exists. While an 1891 uncirculated silver dollar is worth $8,702 at the time of my Google search; the loss of a subspecies of trout cannot be measured with money.

The Silver Trout holds true to the knowledge that Brook Trout match their surroundings. The pond the Silver Trout inhabited is at the foot of Mount Monadnock near Dublin, New Hampshire. The main mineral composing Mount Monadnock and the bottom of the pond is Sillimanite. Sillimanite is not just a mineral that is fun to pronounce, it has the color of tarnished silver. The Silver Trout blended right in with the rocks of the pond.

https://www.usacoinbook.com/coins/3253/dollars/morgan/1891-P/
https://blog.nhstateparks.org/monadrocks-mount-monadnocks-fascinating-geologic-history

-

Aurora Trout

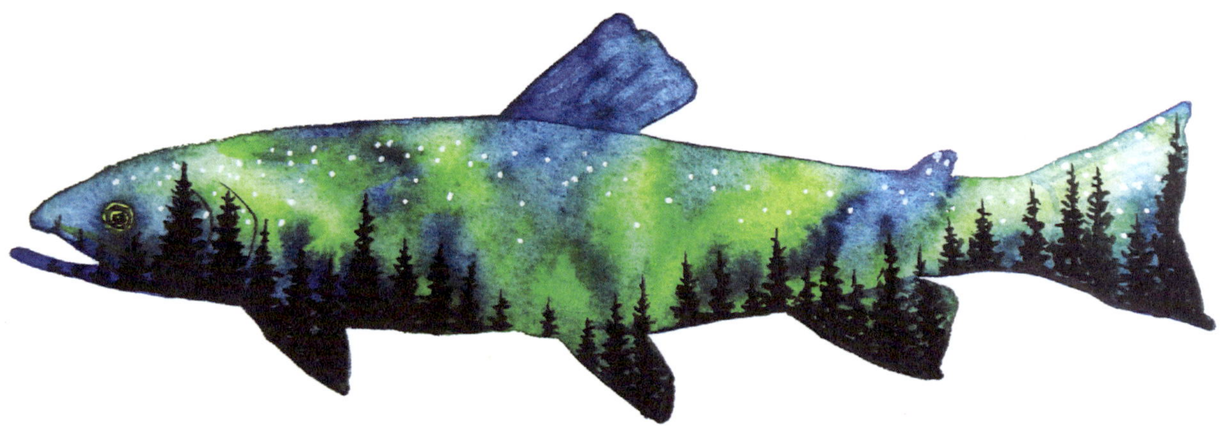

Salvelinus fontinalis timgamiensis

The Aurora Trout is most plentiful in northern latitudes. They vary in color. Colors can be a ghostly white, bioluminescent green, or feathery magenta. All colors fade when removed from the water, leaving a trout that appears to be a rather pale Brook Trout. Some taxonomists believe that the Aurora Trout should not be separated from the Brook Trout and others say it should be called the Pale Brook Trout, *Salvelinus fontinalis albinus*.

In the early 1990's the Aurora Trout in northern Washington state were the ghostly white banded variety, but just a few years later they were a feathery magenta color. It is puzzling how they could all change in such a short time. There are several fisheries graduate students from both the University of Washington and Washington State University diligently working on this question. During the day the graduate students can be found on the lakes, rivers and streams of North-Central Washington and in the evening at bars discussing their finds and plying the locals for tips on catching the Aurora Trout. So far, graduate students from both schools agree The Old Schoolhouse Brewery in Winthrop makes a stunning Double D Blonde Ale and that the Aurora Trout can only be caught in the fall and winter months.

Lake Trout

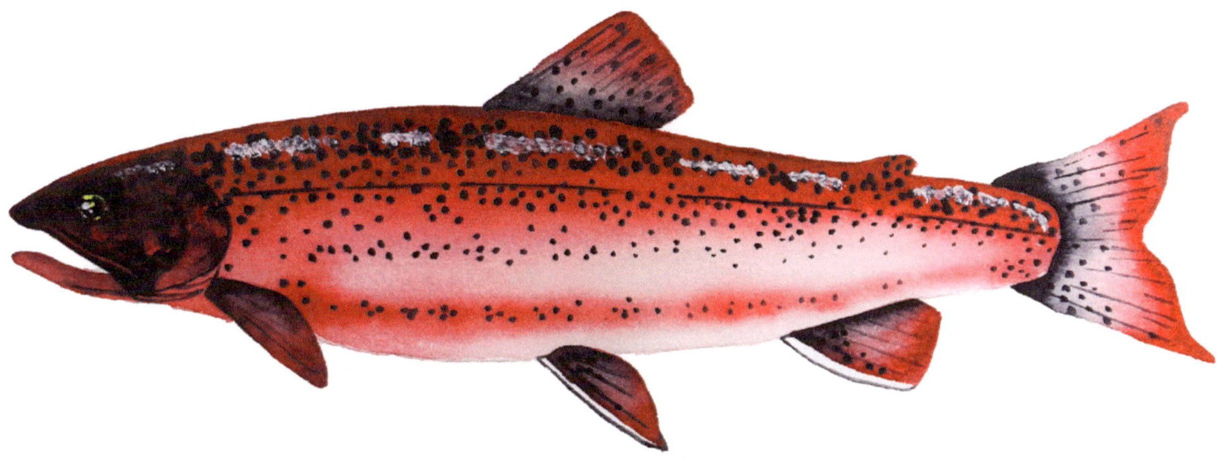

Salvelinus namaycush namaycush

The Lake Trout is found in large lakes of northern North America. While it makes sense that their name is Lake Trout, that is not the naming story I heard. An obscure French painter, Pierre Bisset, traveled west with fur trappers. He arrived at Chiswick House, a Hudson Bay trading post near Great Slave Lake, in 1803. The fishing was great and he stayed, setting up his studio in a one-room cabin dug into a north-facing hill. On days he was not fishing, he painted the local flora and fauna. When running low on supplies he would set up outside the trading post and draw caricatures for food.

One day he caught an extremely large and beautiful trout in red spawning colors that he wanted to paint. As luck would have it, he had run out of the red he needed. As an order from Daniel Smith would probably take 175 years to arrive, because the company was not started until 1976, he had to make his own red. He was also out of cochineal beetles, but he did wear the traditional fur trapper red scarf. Coming from a weaving family (Bisset in French means weaver) he knew to soak a piece of his scarf in wood ash to extract the dye. This red is called Red Lake. He started calling the trout Red Lake Trout after the pigment he used. Over time the name has been shortened to Lake Trout. If you have never heard of the pigment Red Lake, I am not surprised as it is a fugitive pigment that fades over time and is rarely used today. Coincidentally, the Lake Trout's red color also fades quickly when taken from the water.

https://www.nationalgallery.org.uk/research/about-research/the-meaning-of-making/vermeer-and-technique/fading-of-yellow-and-red-lake-pigments

https://www.historylink.org/File9881

httpss://www.gov.mb.ca/chc/archives/hbca/post maps/northwest territories.html

https://danielsmith.com

North of Athabasca: Slave Lake and Mckenzie River Documents of North West Company, 1800-1821. Lloyd Keith. McGill-Queen's Press. 2001

Siscowet Lake Trout

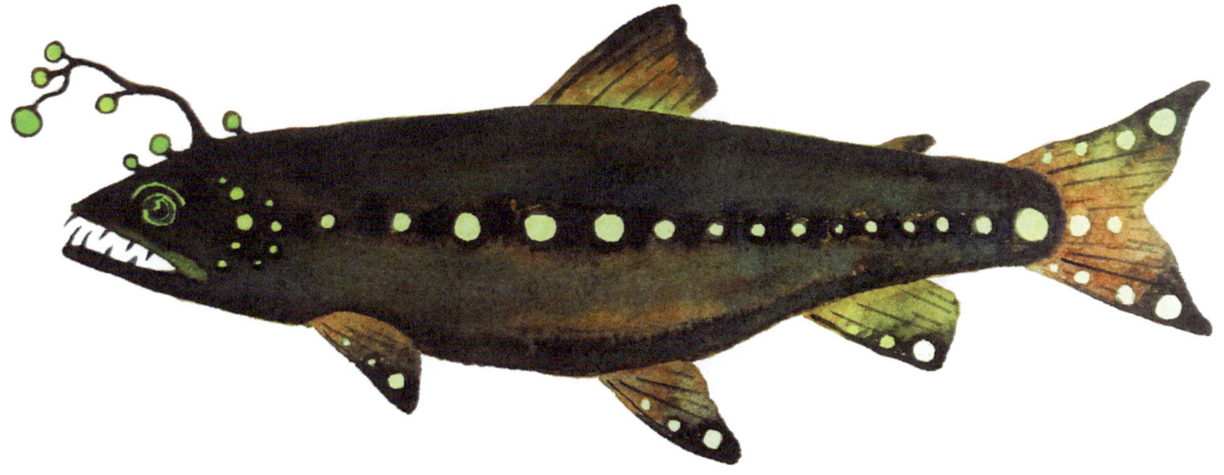

Salvelinus namaycush siscowet (male)

The Siscowet Lake Trout lives in the deepest, coldest parts of Lake Superior. It should not be surprising that it has adapted to the depths in the same way as the Anglerfish has adapted to the depths of the ocean. (This is called convergent evolution.) Tiny lights on "fishing poles" attract food fish which are then swallowed whole by the Siscowet. Sadly, like the Anglerfish, the Siscowet is extremely small. (Learning that the male Anglerfish is only 4 inches long was one of the major disappointments of my childhood.) While small, avid fly fishermen still place the Siscowet high on their must-land list. The difficulty of catching them has made it a much sought-after trout. It takes patience to wait for a small bead-headed fly, the current favorite is a size 18 CB Flashback Pheasant Tail, to sink 600 feet. It takes a lot of skill to detect the strike of this four inch long trout at the end of that much line. There are even a few determined dry fly fishermen who hope to lure one up from the depths during spawning season when the Siscowet spawns in the relatively shallow shoals of 300 feet.

Humper Lake Trout

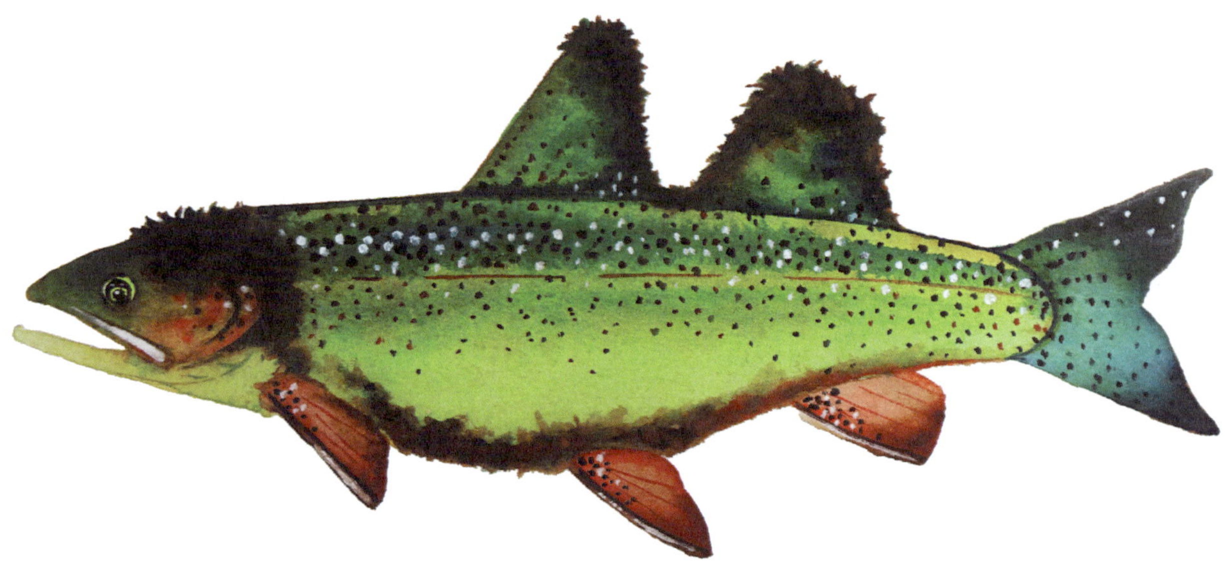

Salvelinus namaycush namaycush

The Humper Lake Trout lives near the large underwater hills in Lake Superior. This trout is only caught during spawning season when they move out of the depths to lay their eggs at the top of these underwater hills. During this season, they become active, striking anything trolled or dropped nearby. One fisherman reported that he lost his last Dry Creek 3.5″ Full Body Double Dipped Tube Jig in Sassy Shad White. He tied on a hook, slip sinker, and the lid from his Beachcliff[R] sardines. Jigged off the bottom, the fluttering lid attracted the ire of very large Humpers.

The rest of the year they live at great depths, hovering just fractions of an inch above the bottom. The extreme cold at this depth has caused the evolution of some interesting survival adaptations. They move slowly along the bottom, conserving energy, siphoning up deep-water worms. Their dorsal and adipose fins have become storage organs for fat giving them the look of a Bactrian Camel. They even appear shaggy. The "shag" is as actually a deep-water algae that covers everything at these depths.

Bull Trout

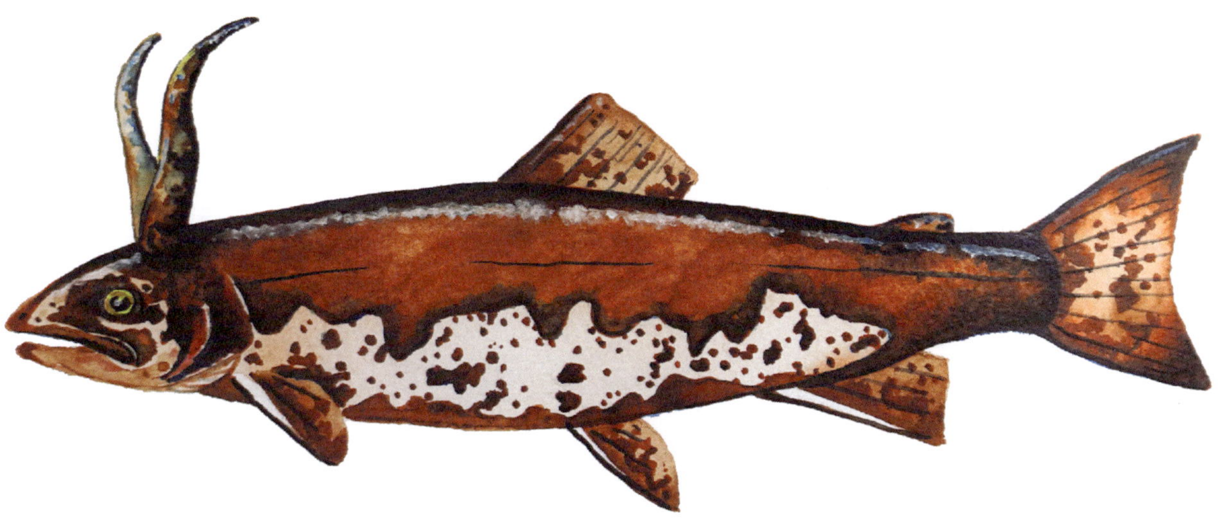

Salvelinus confluentus confluentus (Longhorn variation)

Bull is one of those words like cows that is a collective term and can be used to refer to either sex of these trout. Both sexes are very similar in appearance, but of course they can tell the differences even if the average fisherman cannot. When I was younger, cows came in two types: dairy and beef. All dairy cows were Holsteins and all beef cows were Herefords. I do not know if I was unaware when I was younger or today dairy farmers and cattle ranchers have become more precise in selecting the best cattle for their particular farm, ranch, or market. Today you see cows of all types. The same is true for Bull Trout. The first Bull Trout I caught in a tributary of the Kootenai River had the characteristics of Longhorns. For years, I thought all Bull Trout looked like this. You can imagine my surprise when years later I caught and released one that looked like a Dutch Belted dairy cow. Since then, I have learned Bull Trout come in as many varieties as there are varieties of cattle.

https://www.fws.gov/pacific/bulltrout/
http://www.rioroseflyfishing.com/fly-fishing-blog/blog.php?BlogID=18

Some of the variations of Bull Trout

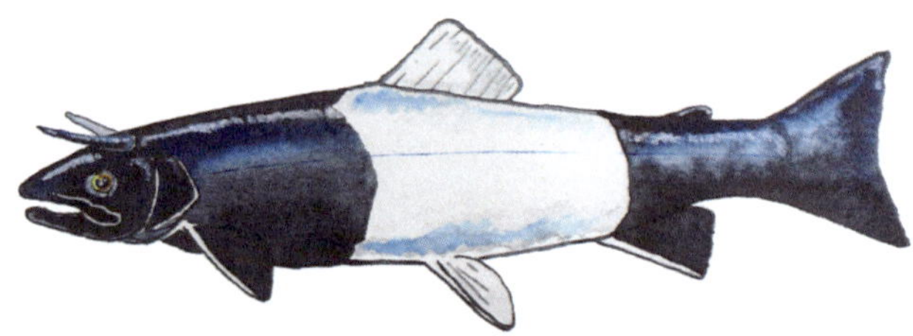

Salvelinus confluentus confluentus (Dutch Belted variation)

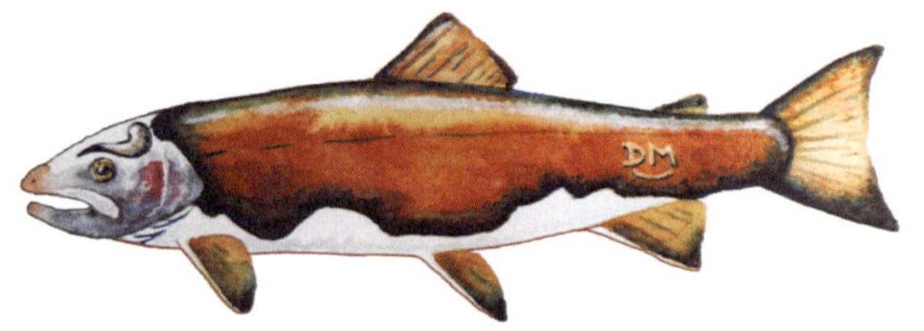

Salvelinus confluentus confluentus (Hereford variation)

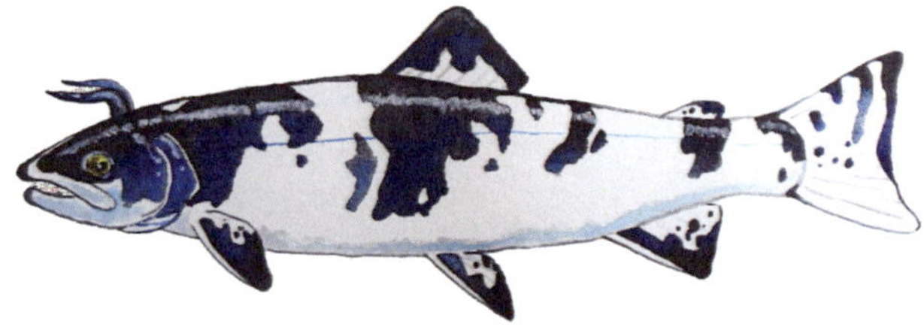

Salvelinus confluentus confluentus (Holstein variation)

Southern Dolly Varden

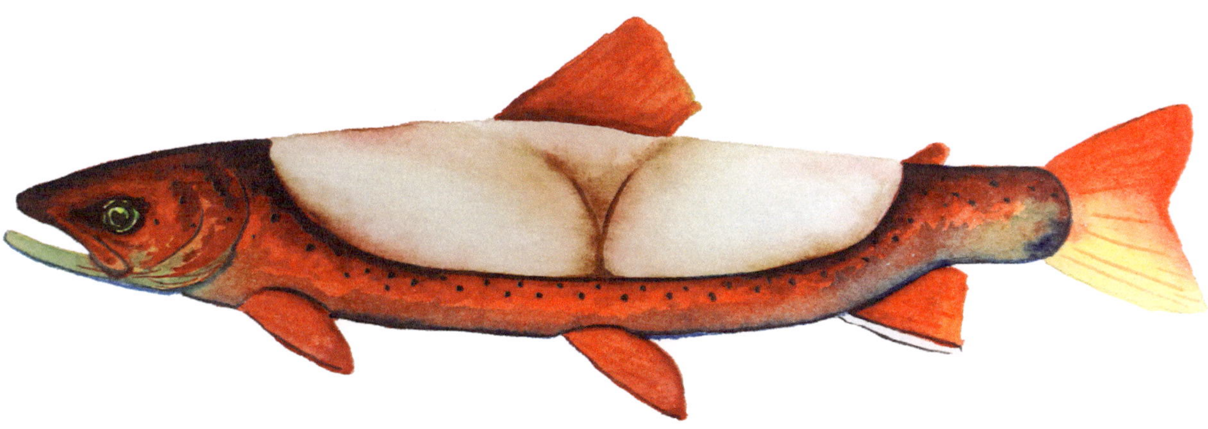

Salvelinus malma malma

Ask any male fisherman above the age of 12 and they will tell you that their dream trout is the Southern Dolly Varden. In reality, fishermen are delighted if they catch any species of trout, heck, even a fish. Most fishermen, when spotting a Southern Dolly Varden waiting in an inviting pool, become bumbling idiots and end up casting into a nearby tree or piercing their ear with a Royal Coachman on a back cast.

Northern Dolly Varden

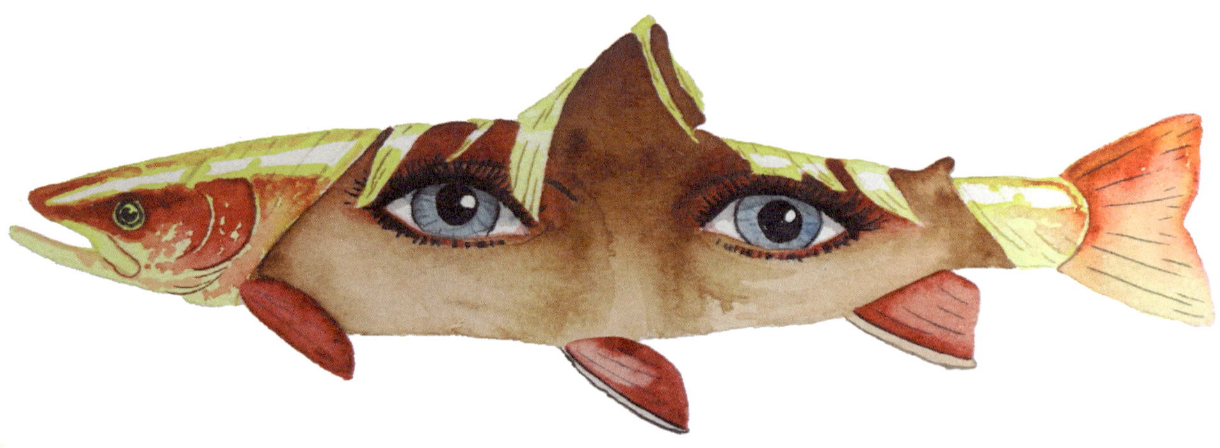

Salvelinus malma malma

There is a Northern Dolly Varden. While not fair or good manners, the Southern Dolly Varden gets the lion's share of attention by fishermen. Unlike most trout that are active during early morning or late evening, Northern Dolly Varden are caught between nine and five.

CHAPTER 2

APACHE, GILA, AND MEXICAN TROUT

My wife likes to play this game: If you could only eat one cuisine the rest of your life, which would you choose. Luckily, I don't have to choose in real life. There are so many great cuisines. Greek, Thai, Mexican and Italian top my list. When she says I have to select one, I always choose Mexican. I am a bit amazed that a few of the same ingredients can be combined into so many different delicious dishes. If I were forced to pick which trout I would fish for the rest of my life, I wouldn't hesitate when selecting this spicy group of trout.

Apache Trout

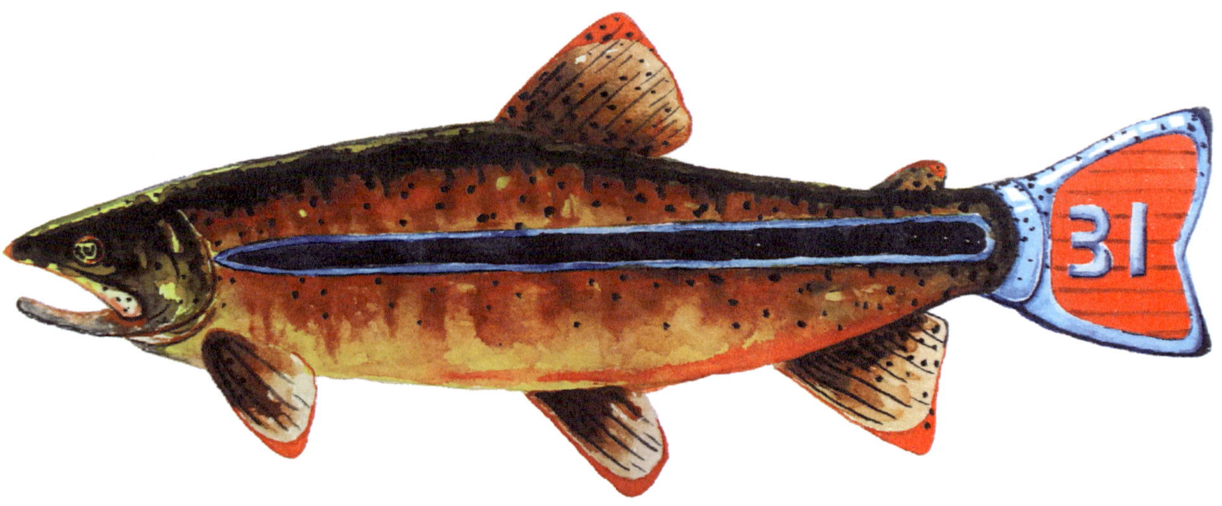

Oncorhynchus gilae apache

Apache Trout are often seen rising for no apparent reason. It has been speculated that they do it just for the *joie de vivre*. The Apache Trout is especially known for its carefree jumps at boat launches, take out spots, and fishing access points. This may explain the uncanny ability of the Apache Trout to mimic the Chevy Apache pickup truck.

It is easy to see why they mimic the weathered Chevrolet Apache pickup trucks. Fishermen of both sexes have a strong attraction to these trucks. The reasons are many and who is to say which is the most important, so they will be listed in no particular order:

1. It is very comfortable to face your fishing partner across the pick-up bed as you share a cold beverage after a day on the river, one foot resting on the step side.

2. You do not have to worry about old pickups getting scratched on rough, overgrown roads.

3. Even though most fishermen should not be so choosey, it is one way to screen potential second dates. If the date shows up in city clothes, wrinkle their nose at the rustic interior of the cab, and ask if your other car is in the shop, you know the spark does not have much chance of igniting. However, if they are wearing worn jeans, smile, say "cool truck", and beg to drive it, you know things are looking up.

4. Attention will not be drawn to your favorite fishing spot as most people will think the truck is broken down along the road.

5. Routine maintenance is minimal and free time can be spent on more important things like fishing and tying flies. Waxing and paint-touch ups are unthought of and a weathered, rusty patina is preferred.

6. The bed is multifunctional. It can help you move. (If you have more possessions than it can carry, it is time to have a yard sale.) It can be that home-away-from-home as you camp along your favorite river or lake. It is a great place to lay back and enjoy learning the constellations on that second date.

7. Fishing rods don't have to be disassembled before stowing and rod tips won't get slammed in the doors.

8. Apache pick-up trucks are an investment, but why would you ever want to sell yours? They are popular with classic car fanatics.

9. They give you a great place to play your old Marshall Tucker eight track tapes. I had a 1950 Chevy pick-up in high school and the eight track was conveniently located facing out, under the seat, just to the right of my gas pedal leg. I could easily reach down and pop in a new tape. Back then it was the Steve Miller Band, Eagles, and Led Zeppelin.

10. People with pickup trucks always have more friends....especially when they need something moved or carried to the dump.

11. Your dog can ride in the back after rolling in that dead thing it found. I think one of my attractions for my wife is that I had a really nice Springer Spaniel and an old truck when I met her. You have to have something that separates you from the crowd.

http://hhclassic.com/n-11535-history-chevy-truck-1955-1962.html
http://www.discovery.com/tv-shows/vegas-rat-rods/
https://classiccars.com/listings/find/1959/chevrolet/apache

Gila Trout

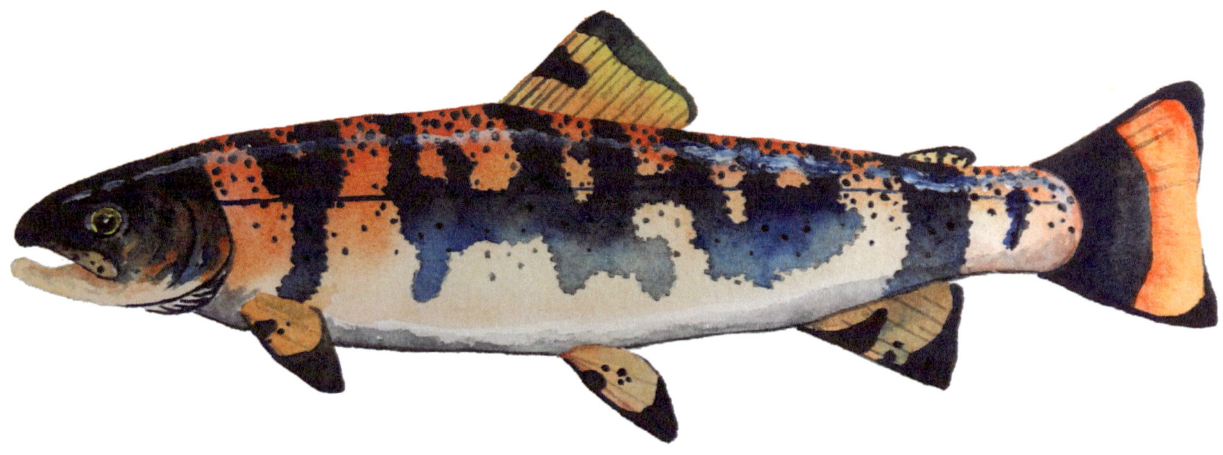

Oncorhynchus gilae gilae

Prior to 1958 the Gila Trout was only found in the upper reaches of a few small streams in New Mexico. Since then, their coloration changed from a goldish rainbow trout to a banded orange and black trout that closely resembles the Gila Monster. Where once Great Blue Herons and fishermen nearly fished them out, they now thrive. It is common to see a heron spit out a Gila Trout in fear and leap into the air. Fisherman cut their line rather than try to manually unhook these deadly-appearing trout. Today its range has extended far downstream.

http://animals.nationalgeographic.com/animals/reptiles/gila-monster

Rio Yaqui Trout

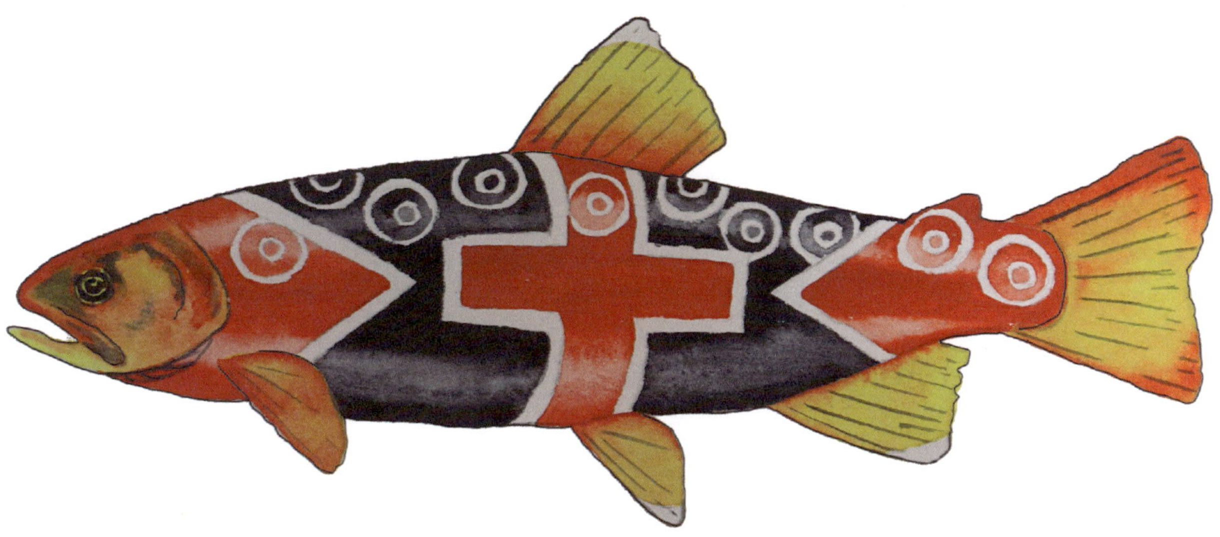

Oncorhynchus sp.

This Mexican Rainbow Trout varies from its *primos* by having a central band of black, red, and white. The Native Americans of the Rio Yaqui Valley were farmers who supplemented their diet with fish. Many of the Yaqui were converted to Catholicism by the Jesuits. For 120 years, they lived in relative harmony. During this time the white and red cross on the sides of the Rio Yaqui Trout gained new meaning. The trout was fished for on Thursdays and cooked on Friday nights. Changing farm practices and the intrusion of settlers and miners to the area affected the numbers of this beautiful trout. Another marking on this trout is the larger-than-typical spots which are strangely similar to the designs found on the Esperanza Stone. While there is speculation that this rock is a message from outer space, it is likely that early Yaqui enjoyed the pleasing patterns on the Yaqui Trout and copied them onto this rock.

https://en.wikipedia.org/wiki/Yaqui
http://atlantisforschung.de/index.php?title=The_Esperanza_Stone

Rio San Lorenzo Trout

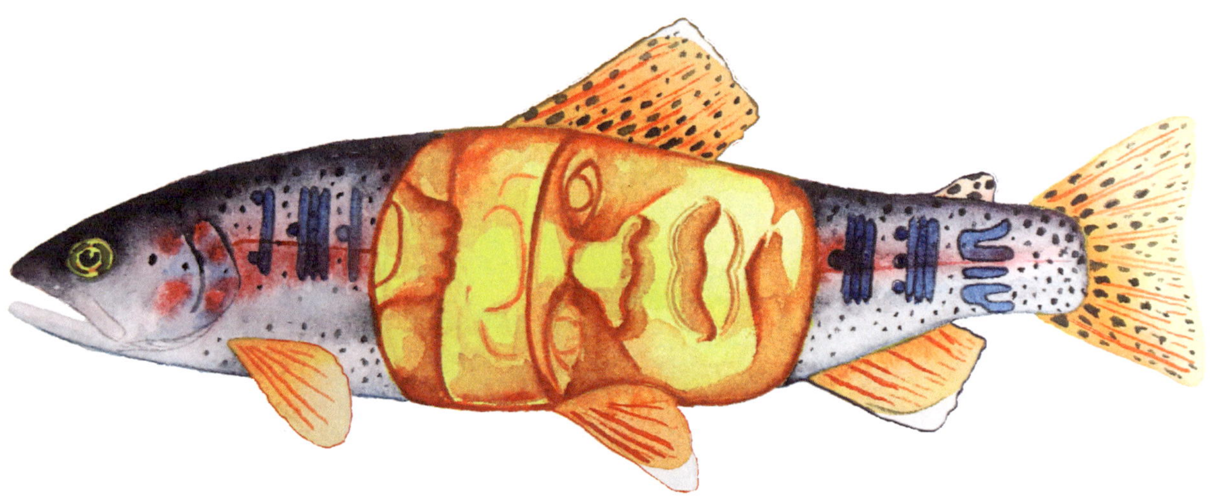

Oncorhynchus sp.

This ancient trout haunts the waters of the Yucatan Peninsula. It is one of the oldest trout, remaining almost unchanged for centuries. Even though the Yucatan Peninsula has seen the rise and fall of several great human civilizations (Olmec and Mayan for two), the San Lorenzo Trout has escaped heavy human predation by inhabiting a unique niche in the trout world. Requiring cool waters, they have found the deep cenotes a wonderful place to live. The tree-lined deep holes keep the water cool and shaded as well as making it difficult for humans to fish. One of the most memorable and beautiful sights I have ever seen was a *pajaro reloj*, the Turquoise-browed Motmot (*Eumomota superciliosa*), twitching its unique tail while perched on a branch above a resting San Lorenzo Trout. It is theorized that these trout move from cenote to cenote in underground rivers cut in the limestone. Ichthyologists believe par marks of the San Lorenzo Trout correspond to the glyphs of the Mayan calendar. The glyphs correspond to the day of the year that all mature San Lorenzo Trout leave the cenotes and enter the underground rivers for the breeding season. The Mayans are thought to have held celebrations on this day. This theory is backed by the sacrificial items such as masks, ceremonial knives, trout shaped ceramics and ceremonial lures found in the cenotes.

Rio Del Presidio Trout

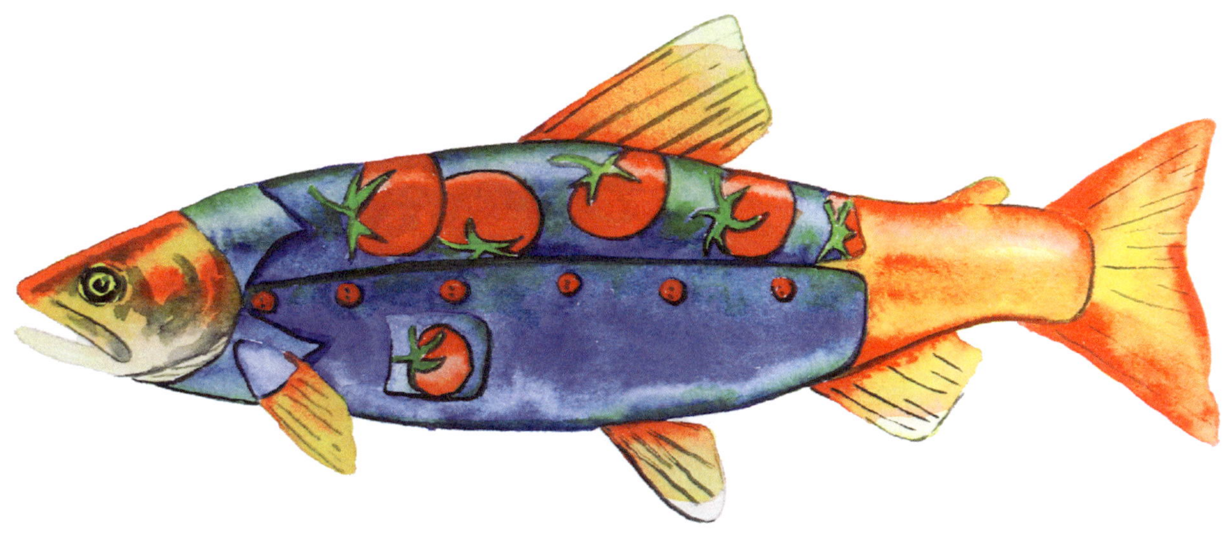

Oncorhynchus sp.

The Rio Del Presidio Trout appears to be decked out in a loose shirt covering its ample middle like many a tourist visiting the Tropic of Cancer. The shirt design appears to be quite fun, covered with the colorful tomatoes that grow along the Rio Del Presidio. In this case, appearances may be deceiving. Follow the Rio Presidio from its mouth upstream and you will see it winds through fields and fields of agriculture and then runs smack into a large dam. This makes it tough living for a trout. I read that the lives of the agriculture workers in this area are pretty tough too.

http://graphics.latimes.com/product-of-mexico-camps/
http://www.redalyc.org/html/1750/175051041015/
https://www.seattletimes.com/business/at-tomato-farms-in-mexico-a-lsquocircle-of-povertyrsquo/

Mexican Golden Trout

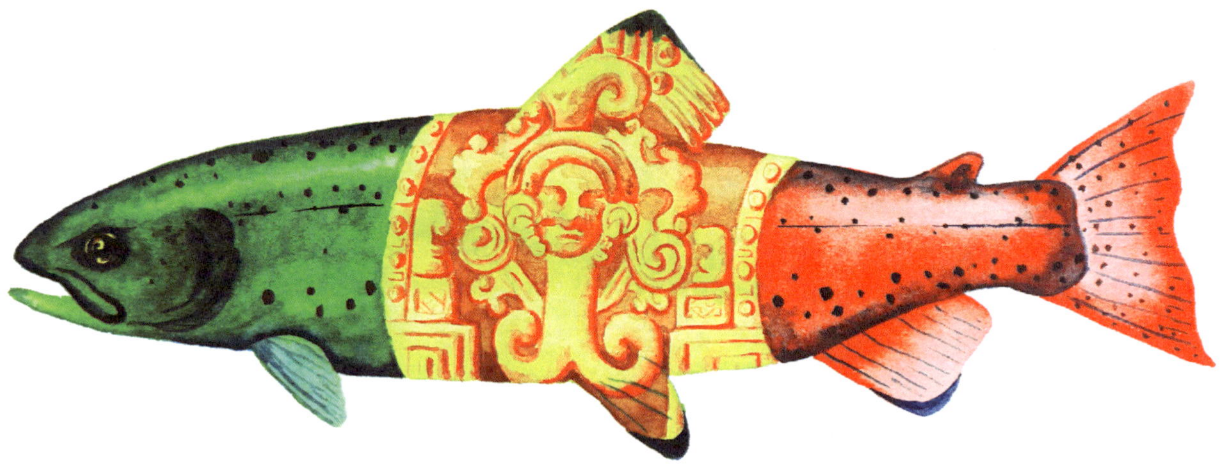

Oncorhynchus chrysogaster

It is a little-known fact that the Mexican flag is based on this beautiful rare trout. The golden band of the trout has been replaced by the eagle, snake, and cactus on the flag. Body bands are often found in nature and serve as warnings. This has been proven with underwater cameras and game cams. The underwater cameras have recorded an indisputable number of predator fish approaching this trout with jaws snapping only to turn abruptly away when the bands come to focus. Game cams above the water show Great Blue Herons stop mid stab and Kingfishers pull out of dives when the bands become visible.

I have had the pleasure of teaching many Mexican students in my art classes. One of the joys of this relationship, besides receiving an occasional home cooked treat or invitation to a *quinceañera*, is hearing about trips to visit cousins in Mexico where they fish with gear that consists of a simple hook and sinker on a line wrapped around a Jarritos bottle.

CHAPTER 3

RAINBOW, REDBAND, AND GOLDEN TROUT

It only seems logical to group the Rainbow Trout with the Golden Trout as any school child knows there is a pot of gold at the end of the rainbow. It is less obvious why the Redbands were included. Perhaps it is from one of those rainbows that are so faint you are only able to see the red band.

Alaskan Rainbow Trout

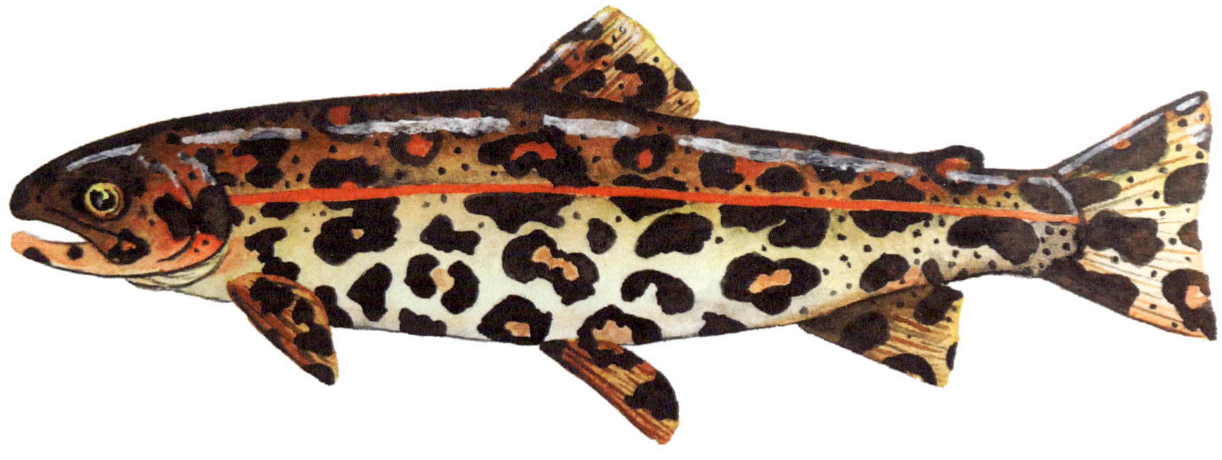

Oncorhynchus mykiss mykiss

The Alaskan Rainbow trout has so many spots it is often called the Leopard Trout. Spots act as camouflage in African cats and you may wonder why a trout that grows to fifteen pounds needs to be camouflaged. Perhaps it is the large brown bears fishing in the rivers that have encouraged this camouflage.

https://scienceillustrated.com.au/blog/nature/how-leopards-got-their-spots/

Upper Klamath Lake Trout

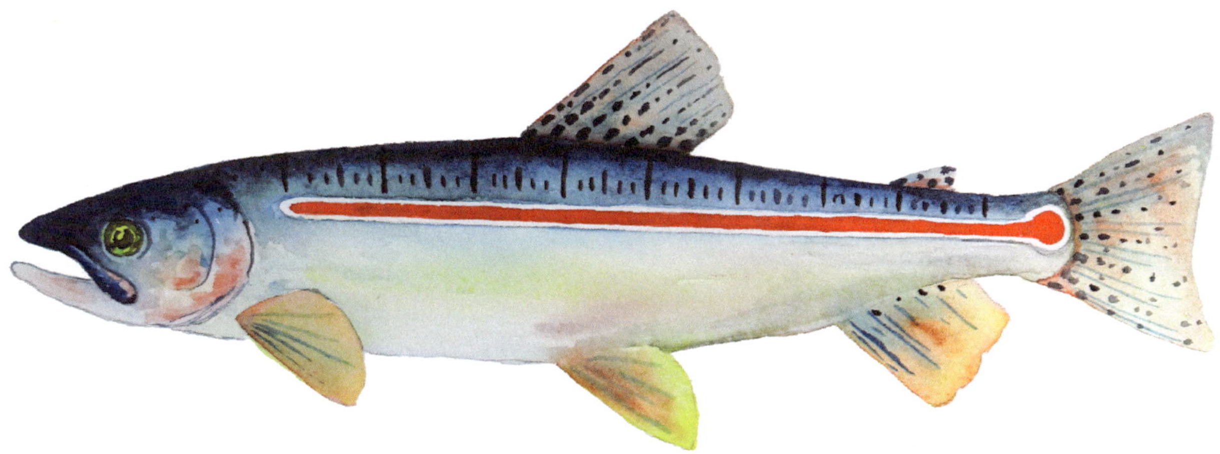

Oncorhynchus mykiss newberri

Upper Klamath Lake can reach temperatures that kill most trout species. The Upper Klamath Lake Trout has physical and behavioral strategies that allow it to survive. Like many a heat stroke victim, these trout do not realize they are overheating until it is too late and they start floating belly up. The other trout notice the victim is starting to overheat. Instead of a red face, the red bulb near the tail starts extending headward, very similar to rising mercury in a thermometer. The heat stroke victim's friends can see the stripe lengthening. They gently guide the belligerent victim into the deepest part of the lake which has accumulated thick layers of cool silt. They gently tuck the victim in up to its gills. Fisheries biologists making SCUBA surveys (one of my favorite acronyms: self-contained underwater breathing apparatus) say summer surveys of the lake look like giant trout sleepovers, with many trout snuggled into the mud.

The pH of the lake is quite high. This has resulted in one of the purest strains of trout in North America. Past attempts to plant the lake with other varieties of trout have not worked because they could not survive the alkalinity.

https://pubs.usgs.gov/sir/2013/5135/section3.html
https://pubs.usgs.gov/sir/2006/5209/pdf/sir20065209.pdf

Great Basin Redband Trout

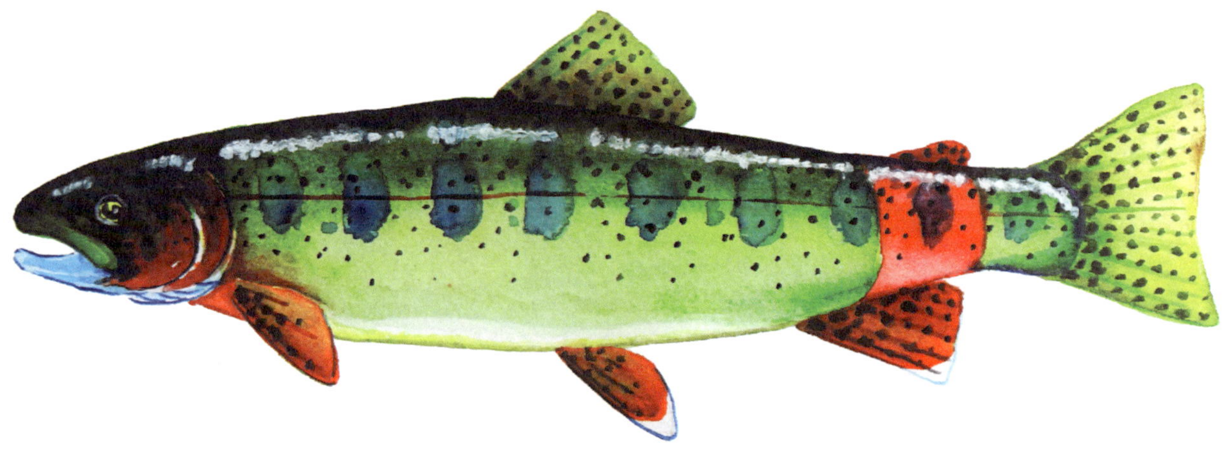

Oncorhynchus mykiss newberri

The band of the Great Basin Redband Trout is much smaller and located posterior to the band of the Columbia Redband Trout. The waters it inhabits are shallower, slower, and warmer than the Columbia River. The band acts by compressing the muscles and enhancing the powers of that part of their body. Being located just in front of the caudal fin, the band enables the trout to make quick bursts of speed to outmaneuver predators in the shallow waters. Prolonged effort in the warmer water would be fatal. There is an inverse correlation between band width and water temperature. The location of the band gives this trout the distinction of being the only trout with a Napthol Red adipose fin. The Lake Trout has a red adipose fin, but it is definitely Madder Lake and not Napthol Red.

The "regular" Rainbow Trout is extremely attracted to this red adipose fin during spawning season and prefers the Great Basin Redband Trout over its own kind. This admiration results in destroying the very thing it loves. Hybrids now exist with half a red adipose fin and no red at all.

Oregon Redband Trout

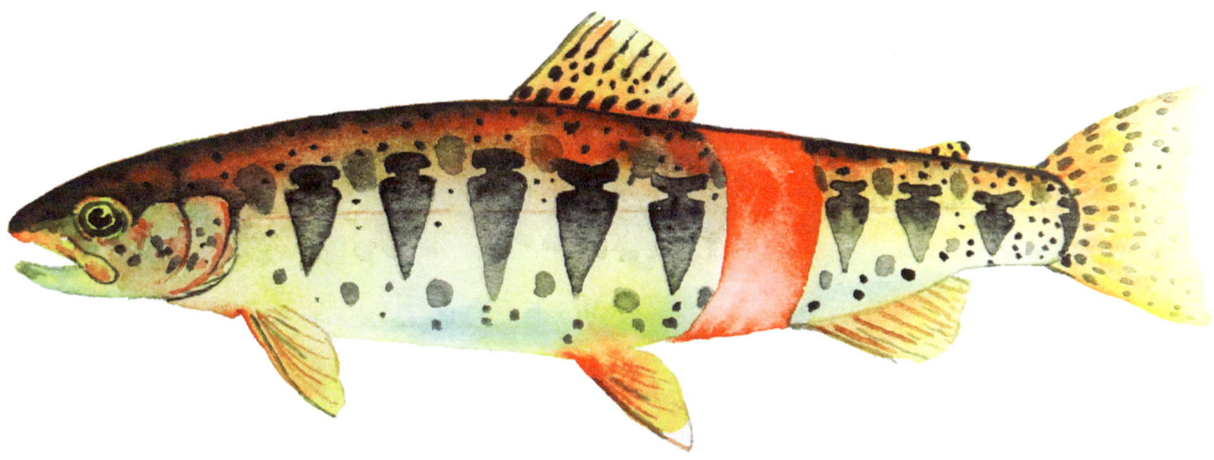

Oncorhynchus mykiss newberri

The red band of the Oregon Redband Trout is slowly moving tailward at about the same rate as its habitat is shrinking. Comparing the location of the bands of the various Redband Trout, one can see a correlation with water depth and water temperatures. These southern Oregon trout are real beauties. Their obsidian-colored par marks have an uncanny resemblance to the beautiful arrowheads made by the Native Americans from this area.

https://myodfw.com/fishing/species/redband-rainbow-trout
https://wildlife.ca.gov/Conservation/Fishes/Goose-Lake-Redband-
Trout#:~:text=Goose%20Lake%20redband%20trout%20are,northeastern%20California%20and%20southeast-
ern%20Oregon.

Sheepheaven Creek Redband Trout

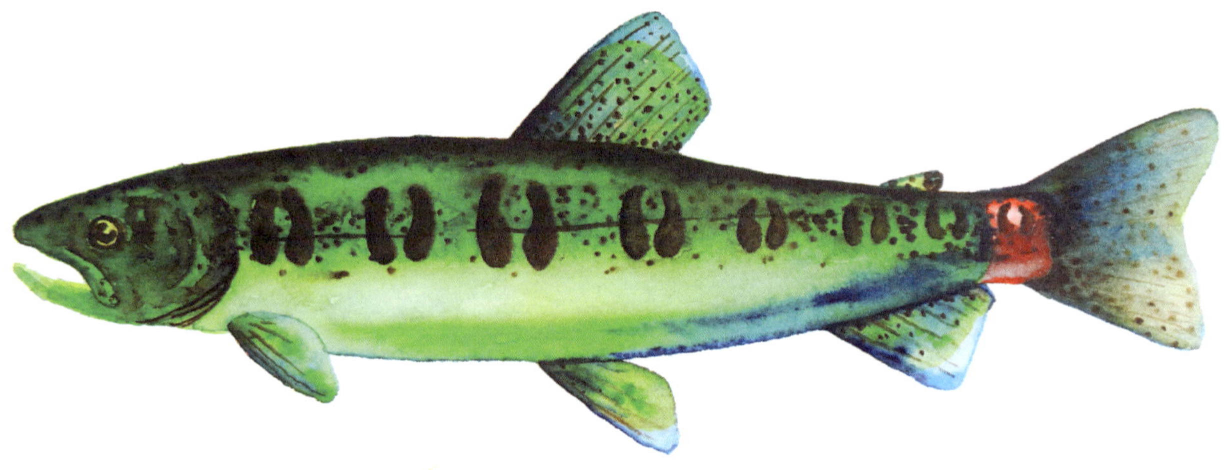

Oncorhynchus mykiss stonei

    If you are fortunate enough to see one of these beauties, you will find that they are covered with blurry brown spots, not unlike sheep droppings in a heavy rain. The par marks have an uncanny resemblance to sheep tracks in the mud. Most of the body is a brilliant emerald green, very much like the beautiful sheep pastures in the Pyrenees, Ireland, and New Zealand. Like the other Redband Trout, there is a red band encircling the body. This particular trout's home is a tiny creek in northern California. It does not need a large band to escape predators. A quick flick of the tail is enough to propel it under a small cut bank or rock. The Sheepheaven Redband has just enough red band near the tail to allow it to survive. A large band would probably launch it out of the creek onto the bank to floppily attract the nearest predator.

    Side notes: I insist on pronouncing creek, "crick". We humans are strange, but as one of my favorite Steve Forbet songs says "...life is strange, but compared to what". Speaking of Steve Forbert songs, another favorite line is "drunk as well", but I always heard it as "drunk as whales". I like my version better as it conjures all these wild images of whales weaving down dark streets singing loudly.

https://www.steveforbert.com/

Columbia River Redband Trout

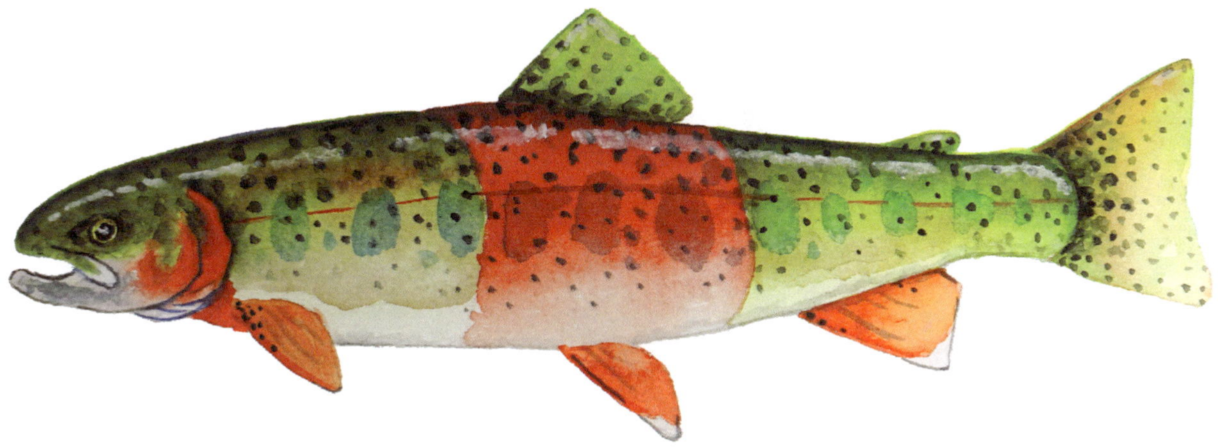

Oncorhynchus mykiss gairdneri

This Columbia River Redband Trout was the inspiration for this book of fictitious trout. When the longhaired Spokane fisherman, Erik Rockliffe, told me about catching Redbands, I had to look them up. I did not know what he was talking about. These were some of the Rainbows I had been catching for years, I just did not know their name. I expected my Google image search to come up with a trout with a big red band around its middle. What I saw instead was a reddish stripe along the lateral line. Well, I could fix that. Now the red band of the Columbia River Redband Trout goes around its middle not along its side. It is a very important feature. The Columbia River is a huge river with strong currents. Historically, the currents were even stronger. In order to move about this river system, the Columbia River Redband Trout developed a band which gave extra strength to the muscles underneath. The band on the Columbia River Redband is larger than the bands of other Redbands because it needs sustained power to navigate the Columbia River and its tributaries.

Steelhead Trout

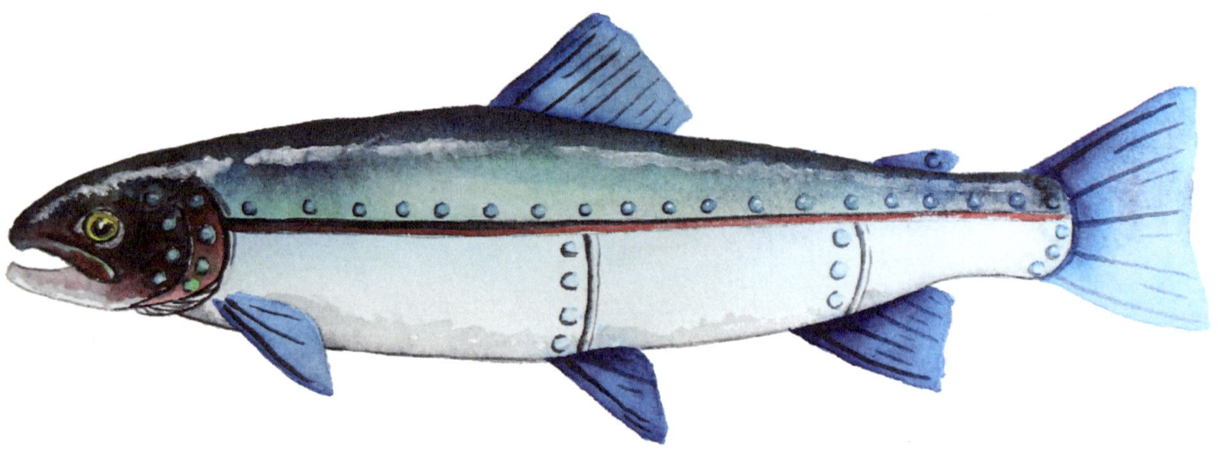

Oncorhynchus mykiss irideus

I admit, my design for the Steelhead Trout is not that inspired. The name literally begs for a literal translation and I succumbed to the obvious. I also am a sculptor and have made my share of steel steelhead. My steelhead design for this book uses rivets for fasteners. They seem more streamline and elegant than bolts. Trout do need to remain streamlined.

Did you know the Eiffel Tower has 2,500,000 rivets? That is a pretty elegant number. If I designed it, it would have some inelegant number like 2,536,491 and 23 left over for some reason. One third of those rivets were inserted on site, some at heights of 984 feet (on a hot day the Eiffel Tower expands to 984 feet and 7 inches). It takes four people to put in one rivet. One to heat it, one to hold it, one to shape the head, and one to hammer it in.

I have caught a few steelhead and have put in many hours for the ones I have caught. Have you ever noticed that the desire to catch something is inversely proportional to the number caught. My youngest brother could care less about fishing (classic cars and Tiki culture are his thing) yet on his first steelhead trip he caught not one steelhead, but two.

https://www.toureiffel.paris/en/the-monument/history
https://www.thelocal.fr/20190516/eiffel-tower-12-facts-you-didnt-know

McCloud River Rainbow Trout

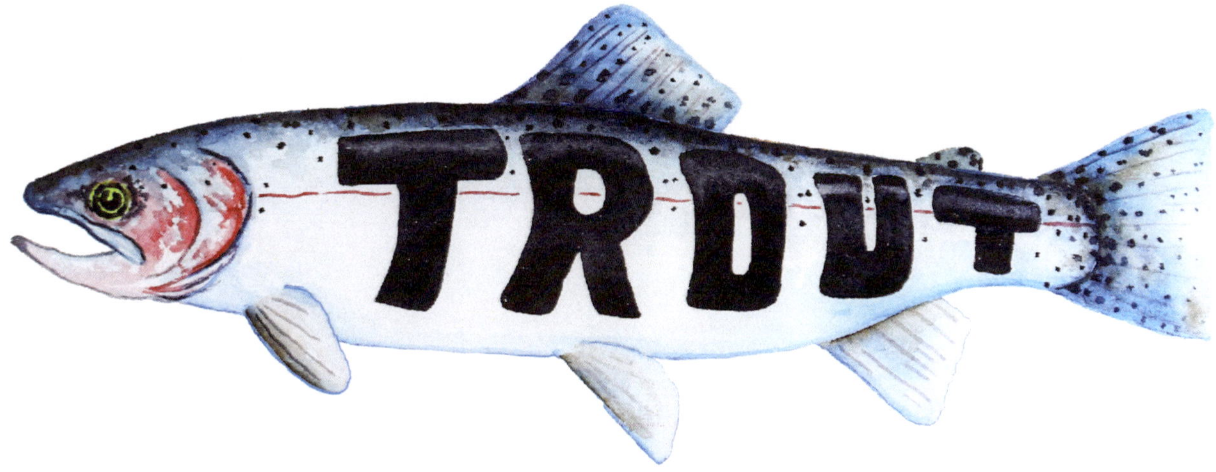

Oncorhynchus mykiss shasta

The McCloud River, where these trout reside, originates in lava tubes beneath Mt. Shasta. This trout, like Mt. Shasta, is pure white with blue shadows and just a hint of crimson on the gills, like a sunset reflecting off snow.

The McCloud River Rainbow has been planted all over the world. If you have caught a rainbow trout, there is a good chance it is from this stock. While a beautiful trout, it is now known as the generic rainbow. Generic or not, a few of these on the grill along with BEER beer makes for a great backyard party after a day on the river.

http://www.mtshasta.com/history-of-the-mccloud-river-rainbow/

Kamloops Trout

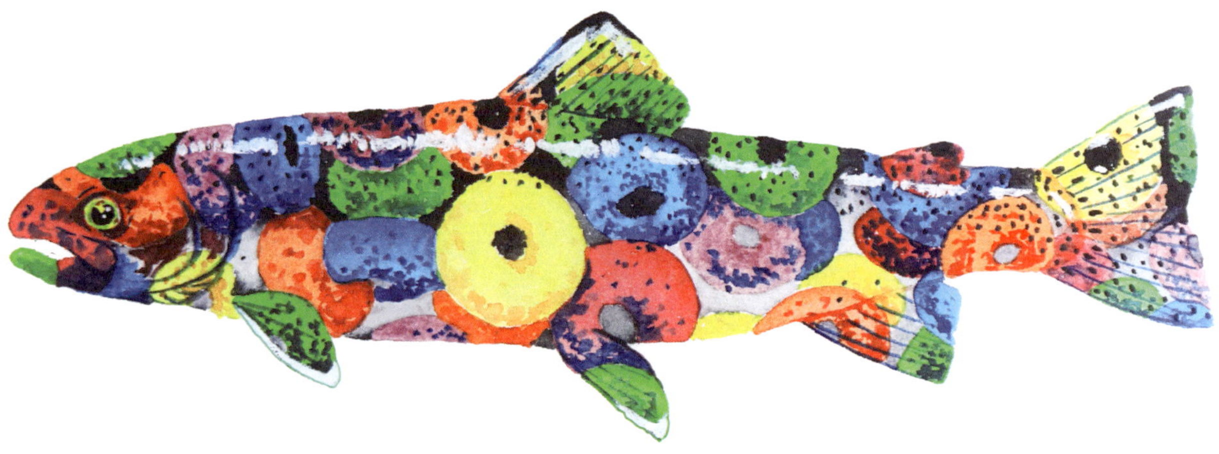

Oncorhynchus mykiss kamloops

Fishermen with young families flock to Kamloops, British Columbia. Kamloops has much to offer families: canoeing, kayaking, whitewater rafting, skiing, ice skating, snowmobiling and plenty of sunshine. However, what better way to indoctrinate your progeny to the fun of fishing than catching these brightly colored trout. They taste good too. Some young fishermen have even been known to pass over their father's slightly burned campfire pancakes drowned in real Canadian maple syrup for these fruity flavored trout. The Kamloops are a favorite of older fisherman who catch so many fish they have to give them away to friends. The unique gastronomic qualities of the Kamloops trout make them easy to give away. The naturally sweet fruity flavors of the Kamloops make them ideal for smoking. All that is required is a smokehouse, no soaking in brine is necessary. Often you can find fisherman smoking them over a hardwood campfire at night while enjoying a cold Kokanee (a local beer and mountain range, not the fish).

http://www.tourismkamloops.com/welcome-to-kamloops-british-columbia

Mountain Kamloops Trout

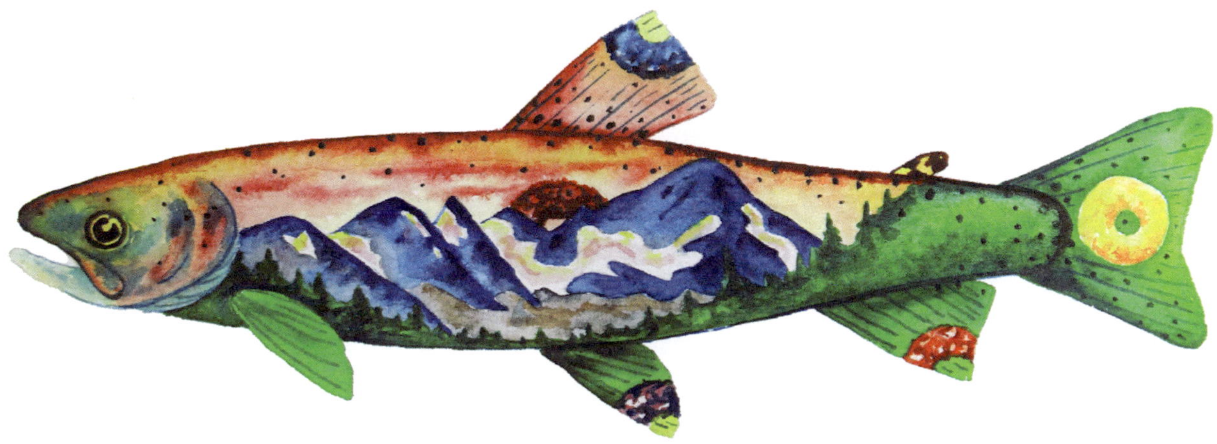

Oncorhynchus mykiss whitehousi

Catching a Mountain Kamloops Trout is a rare treat. Found in the high mountain lakes and drainages above Kamloops, British Columbia, it is not a casual fishing trip. If you live in the United States it requires planning: an enhanced driver's license or passport, ordering a rainbow of Frisky Jenny Flies, and training time for the strenuous hiking you will encounter.

Speaking of rare treats, some of the spots on the Mountain Kamloops look a lot like Froot Loops[R] cereal and I remember while growing up we would get a box on rare occasions. What a glorious morning my siblings and I had. Delicious from the first roof of the mouth scraping biteful to the last slurp of the dyed sugary milk in the bottom of the bowl.

http://www.gameandfishmag.com/fishing/fishing_trout-fishing_rm_aa064504a/
http://www.friskyjennyflies.com/Order_Page.html https://en.wikipedia.org/wiki/Trix_(cereal)

Eagle Lake Rainbow Trout

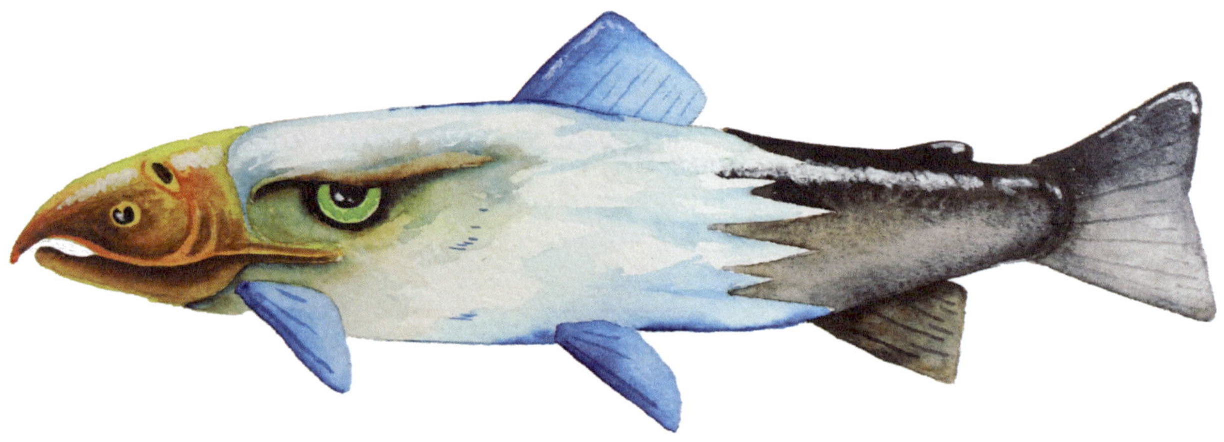

Oncorhynchus mykiss aquilarum (Bald Eagle variation)

Years of evolution in alkaline Eagle Lake of northern California has resulted in two very different phenotypes of the Eagle Lake Rainbow. One phenotype has developed a kype, but unlike most trout, it affects the upper as well as the lower jaw of both males and females. Coloration has evolved into the uncanny similarity of a mature Bald Eagle. While this trout, like its bird counterpart, has a very fierce and aggressive visage, it is a rather calm animal. They prefer to feed on carrion, rather than kill their own prey. They are found hovering among submerged branches waiting for a dead Tui Chub or Western Grebe to sink to their level. They love the spiciness of a Cinnamon Teal.

Scientists do not know if the Eagle Lake Rainbow Trout vocalize. The Bald Eagle is saddled with the call of a large warbler rather than a fierce call required of its fierce appearance. I bet the other raptors make fun of it all the time. Hollywood is great at substituting the call of the Red-tailed Hawk for the call of the Bald Eagle because they think its call is more majestic.

Eagle Lake Rainbow Trout

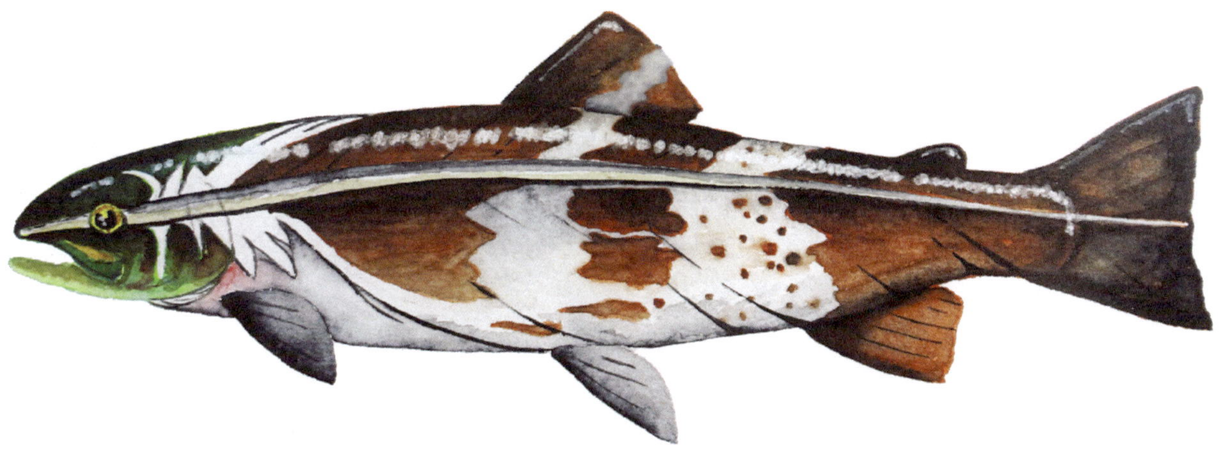

Oncorhynchus mykiss aquilarum (Golden Eagle feather variation)

The other phenotype of the Eagle Lake Rainbow Trout appears to be a molted feather from a Golden Eagle. It prefers to occupy the upper strata of Eagle Lake, like a floating feather, while keeping an "eagle" eye out for any distracted Tui Chub. Their attack is swift and the chub often swallowed whole.

The fishermen of Eagle Lake are divided into two camps based on the phenology of the fish. Bait fishermen prefer the Bald Eagle phenotype which can be caught on a worm on its last legs (leg? Sorry, Richard Scarry). Fly fishermen prefer the strong strikes of the Golden Eagle phenotype. A Pyramid Lake Balanced Baitfish in Tui Chub colors is a favorite fly. It is suggested you use a wire leader to prevent break offs by this unusually aggressive trout.

https://en.wikipedia.org/wiki/Kype
http://www.cawatchablewildlife.org/viewsite.php?site=69&display=q animals of eagle lakes
https://eaglelakefishing.net/
https://www.youtube.com/watch?v=zyujca-1MrM
https://en.wikipedia.org/wiki/Lowly_Worm

Nelson Trout

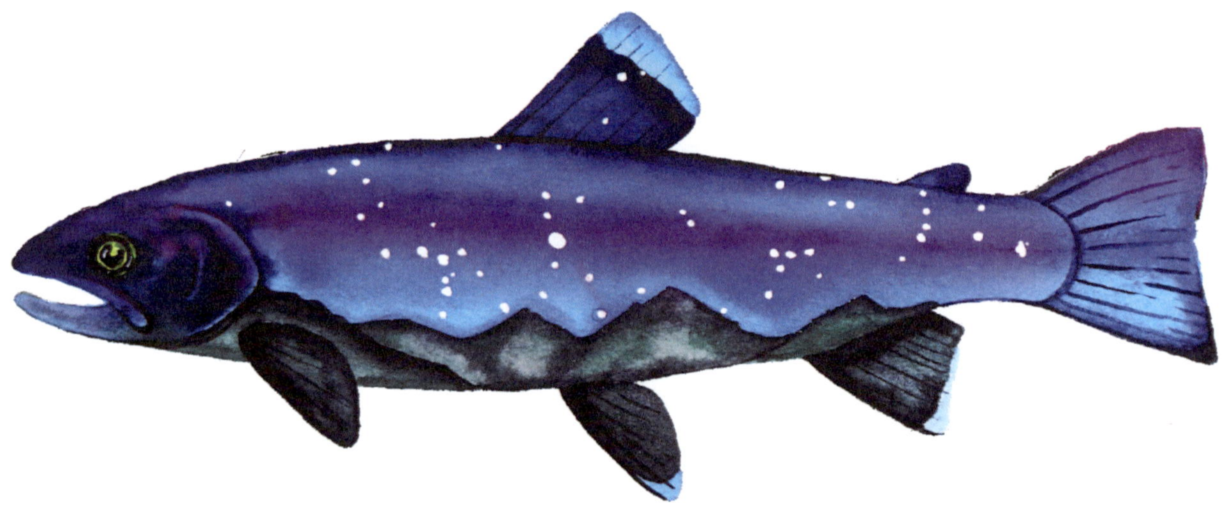

Oncorhynchus mykiss nelsoni

I understand naming a species after the person who first scientifically collected it, but perhaps it should be named after the first people who coexisted with the species or for the region it is from. I am sure Nelson was an upstanding scientist, but the name shouts British Naval Officer or a wrestling move. (Oops. I read about EW Nelson after writing this and he was quite the naturalist and deserves his name on this trout.) Still, I vote for calling it xat xamSi xa7il, the Dog Star Fish. This is a Paipai word, the language of the original inhabitants of Baja California where this trout lives. The dark sky sides of this trout are graced with dazzlingly white spots. You can find the Canis Major constellation among the spots on their sides.

https://en.wikipedia.org/wiki/Edward_William_Nelson
http://www.houstonculture.org/mexico/baja.html
https://asjp.clld.org/languages/PAIPAI
https://en.wikipedia.org/wiki/Automated_Similarity_Judgment_Program

Little Kern River Golden Trout

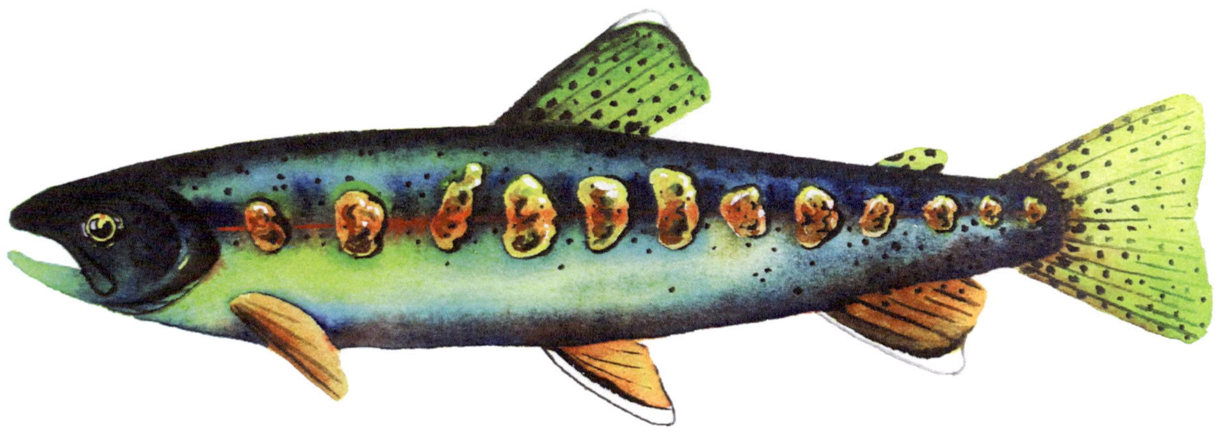

Oncorhynchus aguabonita whitei

It might have been a glimpse of this Golden Trout by a thirsty traveler that encouraged the traveler to set up camp by this delightful river and spend a few days exploring for gold. (As a child I used to love to lay on my belly along any clean looking water and drink to my fill. It has been years since I have done that. Often, I would lay there after my thirst was quenched and watch caddisfly larva crawl along the bottom. Now, surface water is boiled or sterilized in any number of ingenious ways.) Like the Doctrine of Signatures, it made sense to the early traveler that the gold par marks on this trout indicate the river must be gold bearing and sure enough it was. Extraction of gold lasted for a few years, but the real treasure of the area is this enchanting river and beautiful trout. Searching for gold does have its allure, but sharing a campfire with friend near any river is much more valuable in the long run.

Like many things in this world that are done correctly, the kerning on the par marks of this trout often goes unnoticed. However, if you compare it to the par marks of most trout, you can see they have been adjusted just so to emphasize the gold nugget look.

https://en.wikipedia.org/wiki/Doctrine_of_signatures
http://www.goldrushnuggets.com/kerigopr.html

Volcano Creek Golden Trout

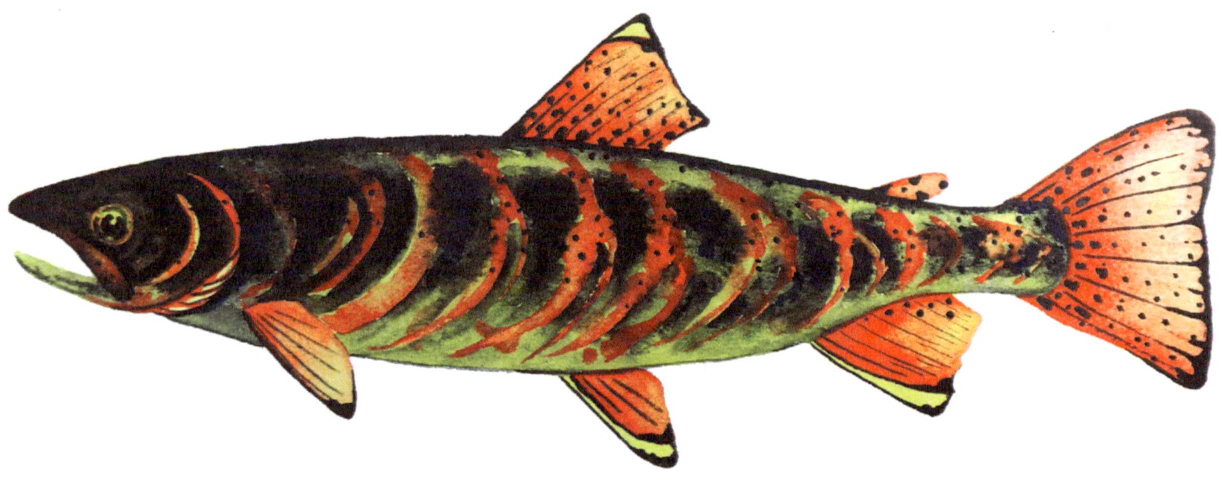

Oncorhynchus aguabonita roosevelti

Volcano Creek Golden Trout are a gorgeous combination of reds, blacks, and yellows in a pattern resembling Pahoehoe lava. This trout pattern probably evolved 5,000-10,000 years ago when lava flowed from the Groundhog Cone. The glacial-cooled waters from the Sierra Nevadas kept the lava from overheating and killing off the Volcano Creek Golden Trout.

https://www.volcanodiscovery.com/golden_trout_creek.html
https://www.britannica.com/science/pahoehoe

South Fork Kern River Golden Trout

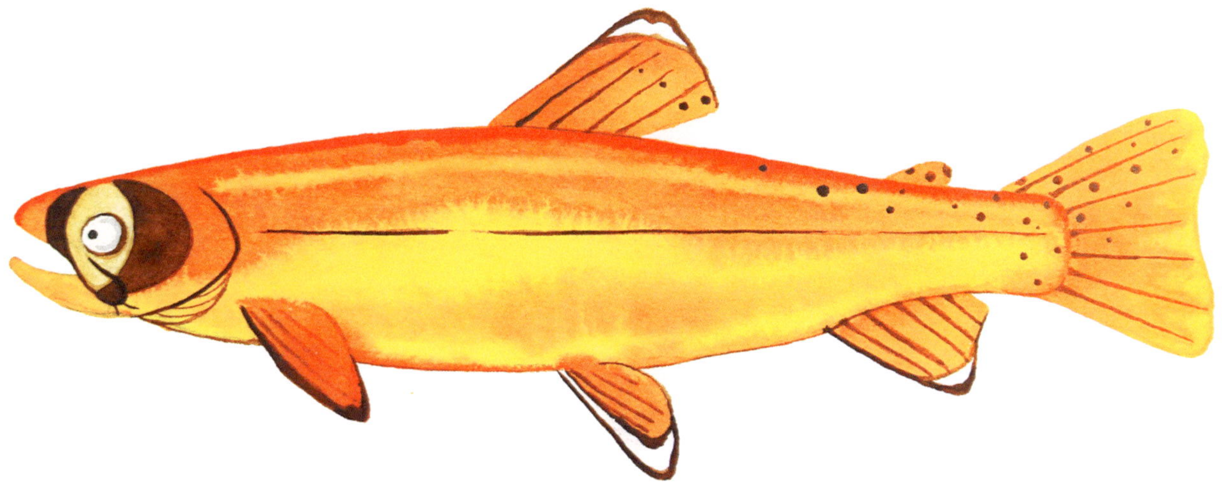

Oncorhynchus aguabonita aguabonita

There seems to be some confusion with the common name of this Golden Trout. While most sources list it as a South Fork Kern River Golden Trout, some list it as a South Park Kenny Golden Trout. I am in the group that believes it should be the latter. Its gold color is more orangey, like Kenny's parka, than gold. Its eyes are rather unusual for a trout. The pupil is constricted like it just took off its dark sunglasses. Another reason I like South Park Kenny better as a name is, like Kenny, this trout has appeared to die out several times. Each time it appears extinct, there is a report that some lucky fisherman has caught another one. In recent years, this cycle of dying off and making a comeback has slowed down and with luck, fishermen for generations will enjoy catching this beauty. (I really like the scientific name of this trout. It translates to *Hooked Snout beautiful water beautiful water.*)

http://southpark.wikia.com/wiki/Kenny_McCormick

Gilbert Golden Trout

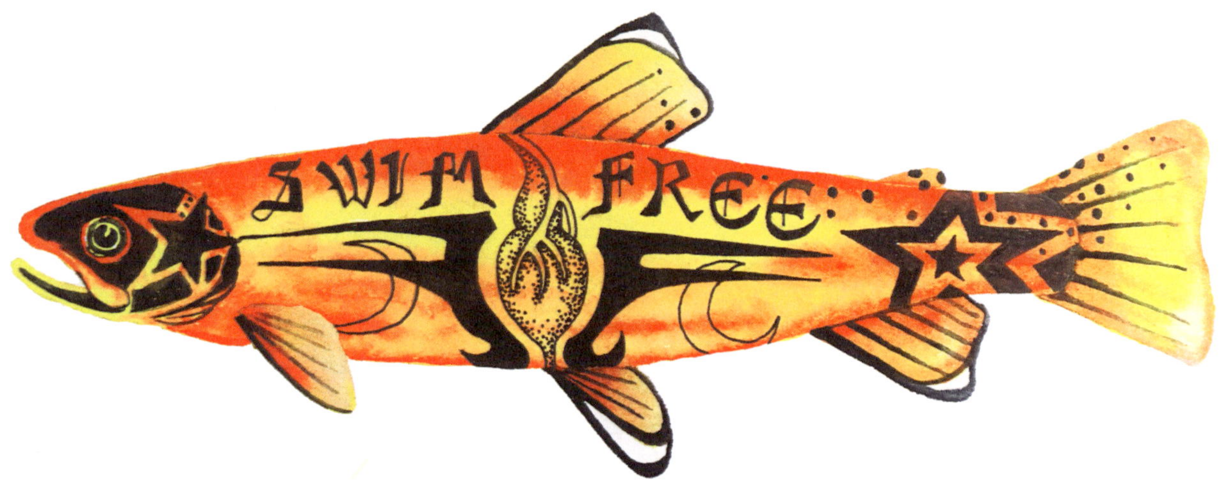

Oncorhynchus aguabonita gilberti

Most fisheries biologists believe that the Gilbert Golden Trout is named after pioneer ichthyologist Charles Henry Gilbert. It would be a fitting tribute to the man who described 620 species of fish. Most fishermen believe it is named after the Dutch mixed martial artist Gilbert Yvel. The markings do not match the tattoos of Yvel, but its fighting style does. It is a strong fish that does not pull any punches. It has brute strength and lightning quick runs.

https://whttps://en.wikipedia.org/wiki/Gilbert_Yvel

CHAPTER 4

CUTTHROAT TROUT

Cutthroat is a rather harsh name for such a beautiful group of trout. The person responsible for naming this group must have subscribed to the tabloid school of journalism. True, the red mark under the jaw is a distinguishing feature. Perhaps Western Trout, Red Bandana Trout, or Rosacea Trout would be a more elegant name. On second, thought, I bet the name Cutthroat Trout sells more fishing magazines, flies, and guided trips.

Colorado River Cutthroat Trout

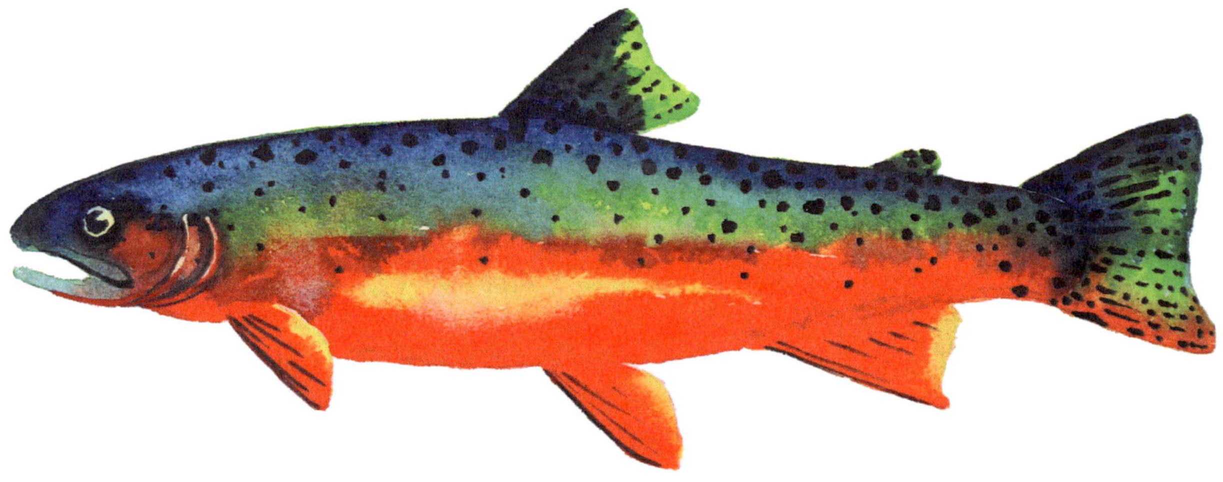

Oncorhynchus clarkii pleuriticus

Compared to the other trout in this book, the Colorado River Cutthroat Trout is a normal looking trout. It looks like a spawning male Colorado Cutthroat Trout, but not exactly. Over eons this trout has learned how to perfectly mimic the incredible Colorado sunsets reflected on the river's surface in order to hide in plain sight from fishermen .

The Colorado River Cutthroat Trout enjoy a hearty breakfast of large terrestrials like beetles and grasshoppers. They skip lunch in the heat of the day and have a *merienda* of mayfly and caddisfly snacks around five. As the sun sets, they gather midstream and float on their sides, one eye skyward to look for the green flash followed by one of Colorado's magnificent sunsets. The sides of this trout slowly shift colors with the sky. After the last color has faded from the sky and the stars have "tumbled out, neck and crop" (Robert Service: "The Spell of the Yukon") they right themselves and slip into the inky depths of the river for *tapas* of assorted nymphs.

https://news.orvis.com/fly-fishing/fish-facts-colorado-river-cutthroat-trout-oncorhyncus-clarkii-pleuriticus#:~:text=They%20are%20opportunistic%20feeders%2C%20focusing,specimens%20will%20eat%20smaller%20fish.

Greenback Cutthroat Trout

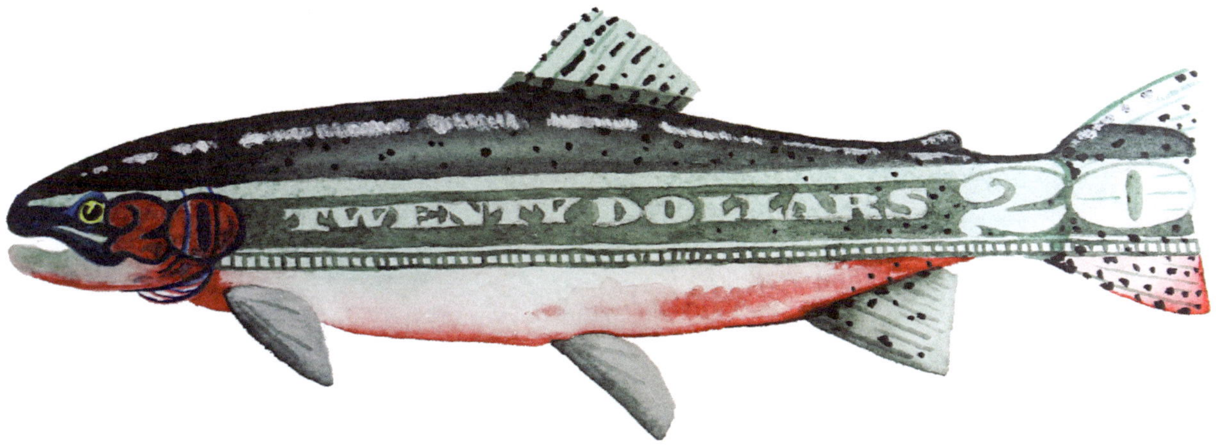

Oncorhynchus clarkii stomias

When droves of miners flowed into Colorado in search of gold, they did not always find it. However, the hungry miners panning the cold-water tributaries of the South Platte and Arkansas Rivers did find Greenbacks. The miners ate them almost into extinction. The Greenback Cutthroat Trout the miners of Colorado caught were in denominations of 1 US dollar. Even though the Greenbacks have survived near extermination by overharvesting, hybridization with rainbow trout, and competition with brook trout, they have not survived inflation. Today the marks of the Greenback are of the US twenty-dollar bill.

https://historytogo.utah.gov/pikes-peak/
https://www.safeway.com/shop/search-results.html?q=flour

Yellowfin Cutthroat Trout

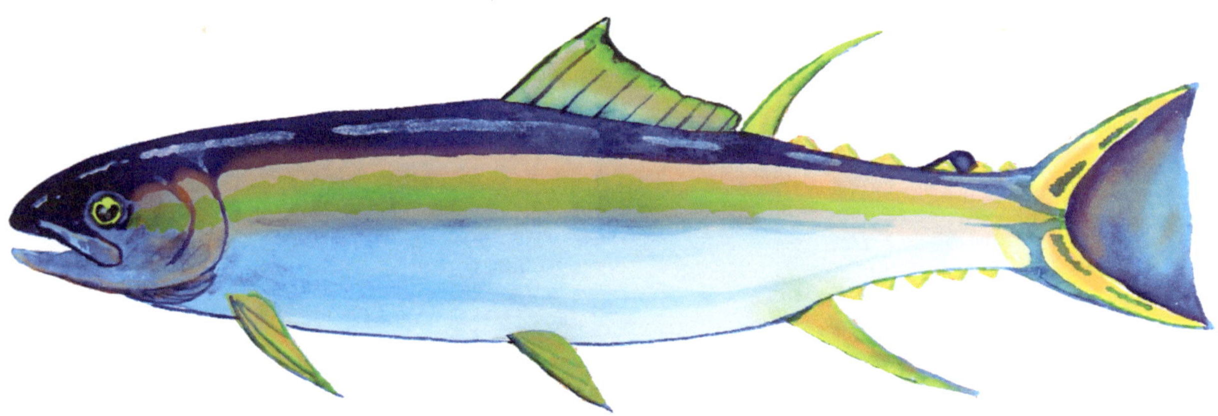

Oncorhynchus clarkii macdonaldi

The Yellowfin Cutthroat Trout was given its name because of its physical similarity to the Yellowfin Tuna. Fossil records reveal the Yellowfin Cutthroat Trout grew to 7 feet in length. Historical reports state that the similarities do not stop at looks.

"It struck with such ferocity the rod was almost yanked from my arms. In a matter of seconds, I was down to my backing. Luckily, I was fishing in a light boat. Rather than snapping my line, it towed my boat around the lake for nearly 3 hours before I landed it" recorded early fisherman Joe Black of Colorado Springs.

It may be hard to believe that this trout once swam the waters of the mountainous, inland state of Colorado. The Colorado of the Pliocene and Pleistocene looked much different than it does today. Huge lakes covered Colorado. The Yellowfin Cutthroat Trout migrated back and forth from these lakes to the Sea of Cortez. Spending part of their lives in the rich Sea of Cortez allowed them to grow to great size. Climate change shrunk the lakes, trapping them inland, and in time, to become extinct.

http://oceana.org/marine-life/ocean-fishes/yellowfin-tuna
https://pubs.usgs.gov/of/2007/1193/pdf/OF07-1193_ChG.pdf

Rio Grande Cutthroat Trout

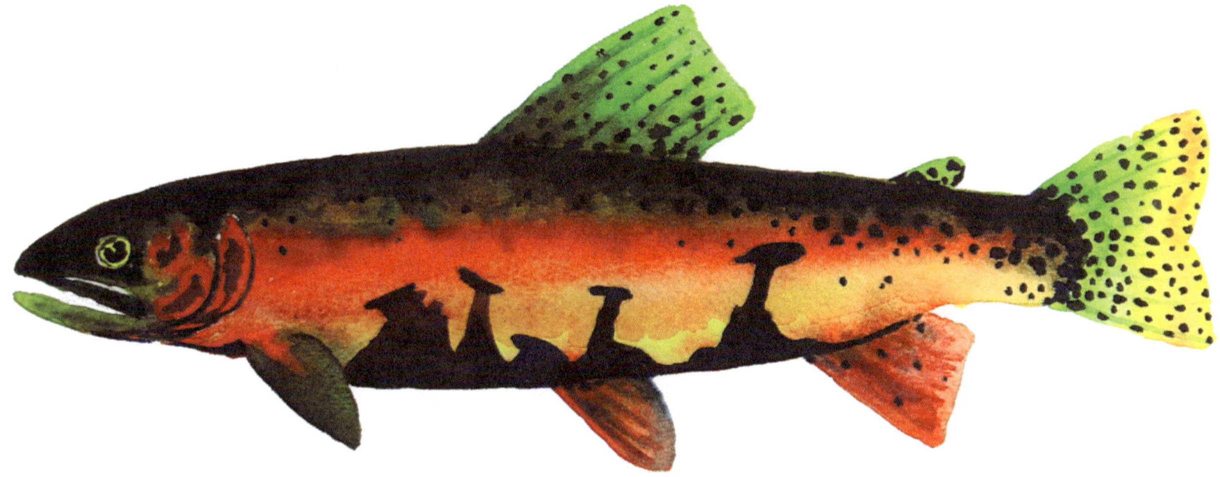

Oncorhynchus clarkii virginalis

The glorious sunset sides of this beautiful cutthroat have earned it the title of the State Fish of New Mexico, beating out less flashy contestants like the Rio Grande Sucker. However, it is the threatened status of the Rio Grande Silvery Minnow that has ecologists fighting to keep the Rio Grande River full of water.

The Rio Grande Cutthroat Trout plays its role well in promoting tourism to the Land of Enchantment. In addition to mimicking New Mexico sunsets on its sides, state landmarks appear silhouetted against the reds and yellows. This particular trout shows the Ah-Shi-Sle-Pah hoodoos. Other fish sport images of Shiprock, White Sands, Ghost Ranch, Carlsbad Caverns and Valles Caldera.

http://www.americansouthwest.net/highlights/hoodoos/18.html
http://www.wildlife.state.nm.us/fishing/native-new-mexico-fish/
https://www.newmexico.org/things-to-do/nature/places-to-visit-and-photograph/
https://www.hcn.org/issues/47.13/does-the-fate-of-the-silvery-minnow-foretell-the-future-of-the-rio-grande

Pecos Strain of the Rio Grande Cutthroat Trout

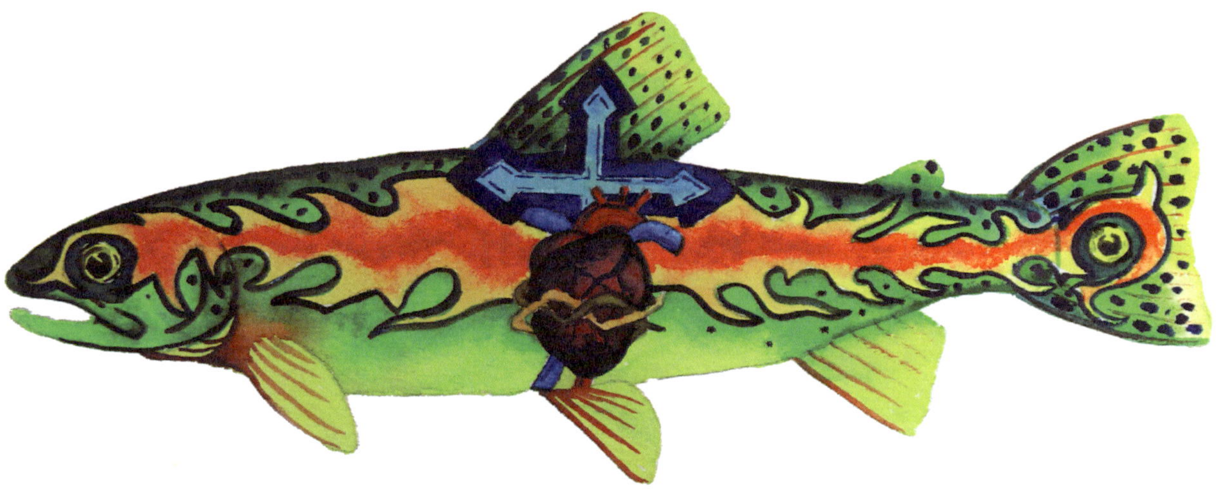

Oncorhynchus clarkii virginalis

The Pecos River joins the Rio Grande River north of Del Rio, Texas. Its headwaters are in the Sangre de Cristo Mountains. Myth has it that Spanish explorers were out of food when they stumbled upon the Pecos River. They were not prepared for fishing. They carried harquebuses, lances, and swords. Lucky for them, many cutthroat were stranded in a side channel. It was as easy as harquebusing fish in a barrel to harvest them. Their tag-a-long myopic Franciscan monk mistook the red spot on the trout's side for the sacred heart of Christ. He declared their salvation a miracle and named the mountains the Sangre de Cristo (Blood of Christ) Mountains.

As a kid I attended a church called Sacred Heart. It had a heart carved into the lintel above the main door. I always read it as the scared heart and thought it was scary to have a human heart above the doorway.

https://www.thoughtco.com/armor-and-weapons-of-spanish-conquistadors-2136508

Lahontan Cutthroat Trout

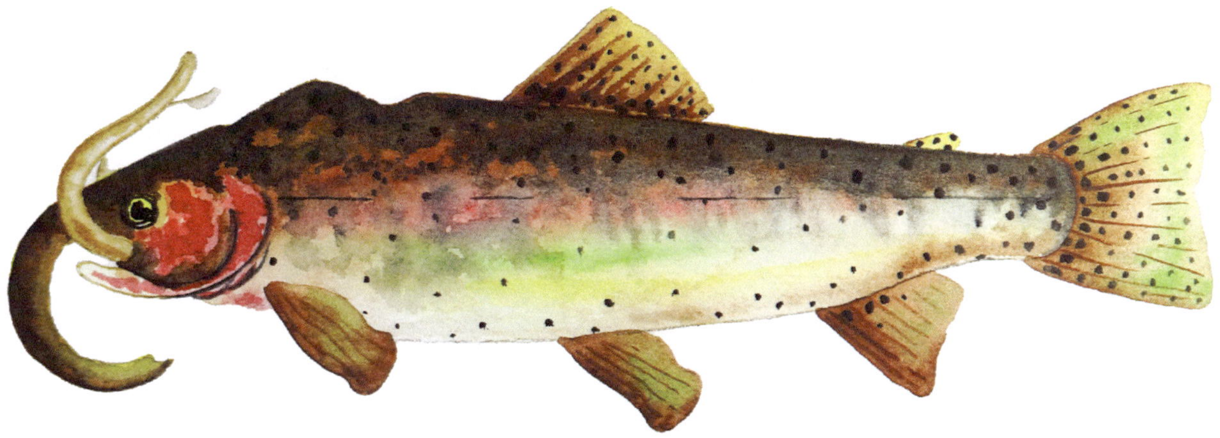

Oncorhynchus clarkii henshawi

It is hard to image the arid state of Nevada underwater. During the Pleistocene it was covered by Lake Lahontan, a 900-foot deep, 86,100 square mile lake. This is where the Lahontan Cutthroat Trout evolved and roamed. In the mineral rich waters this trout grew to enormous size. Fossil records indicate they grew up to 200 feet in length with a weight of 7 tons. Like most of the Earth's giant animals it was a plant eater, eating phytoplankton that thrived on the surface of ancient Lake Lahontan. It is believed its long proboscis allowed it to siphon phytoplankton from the surface while it was able to stay in the cooler depths.

The climate changed and Lake Lahontan dried up into what is now alkaline Pyramid Lake. The Lahontan Trout shrunk in size and became alkaline tolerant. Today, Lahontan Cutthroat Trout have been planted in alkaline lakes throughout the West.

I was introduced to the Lahontan Cutthroat Trout in the 1980's at Lake Lenore in Washington State. At that time, my wife worked in the produce department of John's Thrift Grocery Store in the nearby town of Soap Lake. I could pick her up on her 5 PM dinner break, drive to Lake Lenore and catch several 6-pound Lahontans and have her back to work by 6 PM. At first, I used expired broccoli pieces from the produce department and a #18 hook with a split shot and bobber. Once I realized how easy they were to catch, I switched to a fly rod and this cute little fly I designed called the Vibrant Volvox. (A Volvox is a freshwater algae that forms a hollow spherical colony of up to 60,000 cells.) To make this fly, Peacock hurl is wrapped into a ball on a #24 hook and short strands of neon green Flashabou Holographic Tinsel are inserted into the ball to resemble flagella.

https://www.britannica.com/science/Volvox
http://www.onlinenevada.org/articles/ice-age-nevada-and-lake-lahontan
https://news.orvis.com/fly-fishing/fish-facts-lahontan-cutthroat-oncorhynchus-clarki-henshawi
https://twistedsifter.com/2012/04/15-of-the-largest-animals-in-the-world/

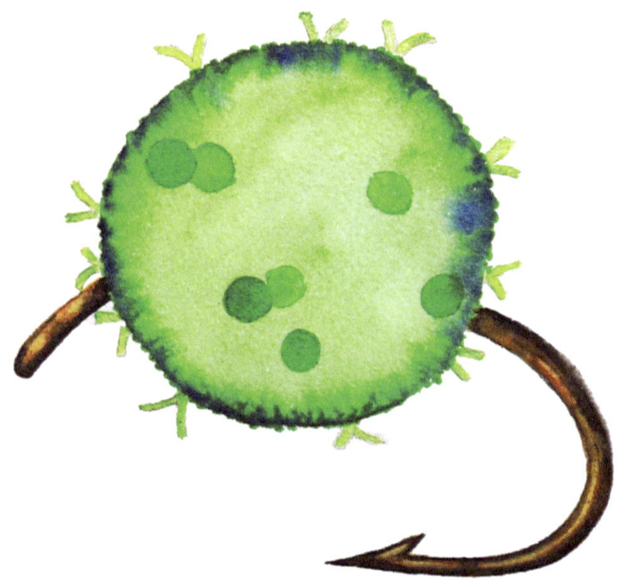

Vibrant Volvox
*Materials: yarn or peacock hurl and your favorite flash
material*

Paiute Cutthroat Trout

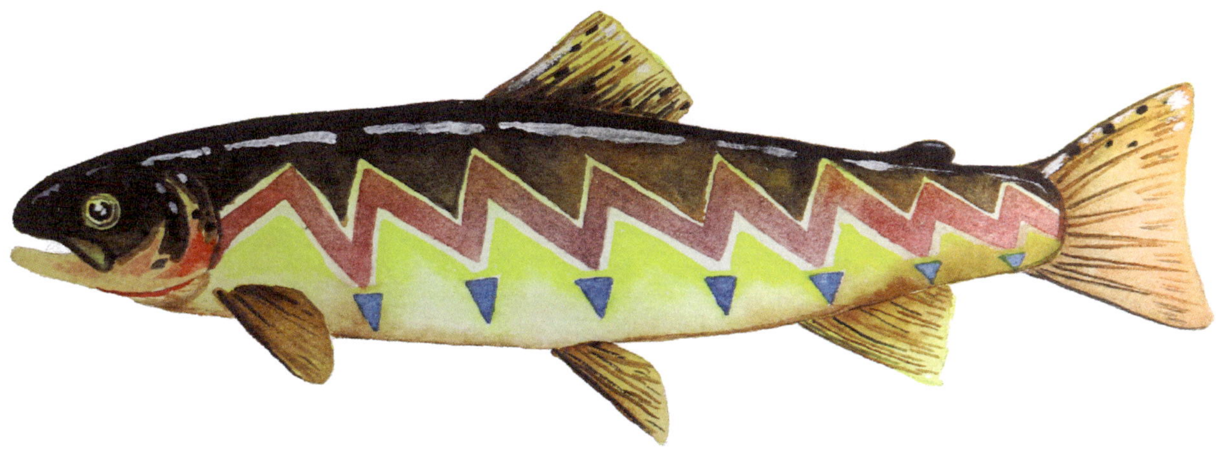

Oncorhynchus clarkii seleiris

The Paiute Cutthroat Trout carries the markings of the wonderful basket maker Tina Charlie (1869-1962). She was one of the winners of the basket competitions at the last Indian Field Day sponsored by the Yosemite Park Service in 1929. She was a creative basket maker and made some of the first documented negatively patterned baskets. Her baskets incorporate sedge root, redbud, and bracken fern. I based my trout design on a basket by Tina Charlie and was delighted to find the real Paiute Cutthroat Trout is basket-colored with nice warm browns and soft pinks.

https://en.wikipedia.org/wiki/Tina_Charlie
https://yosemitemonolakepaiute.wordpress.com/category/mirror-lake/page/2/

Alvord Cutthroat Trout

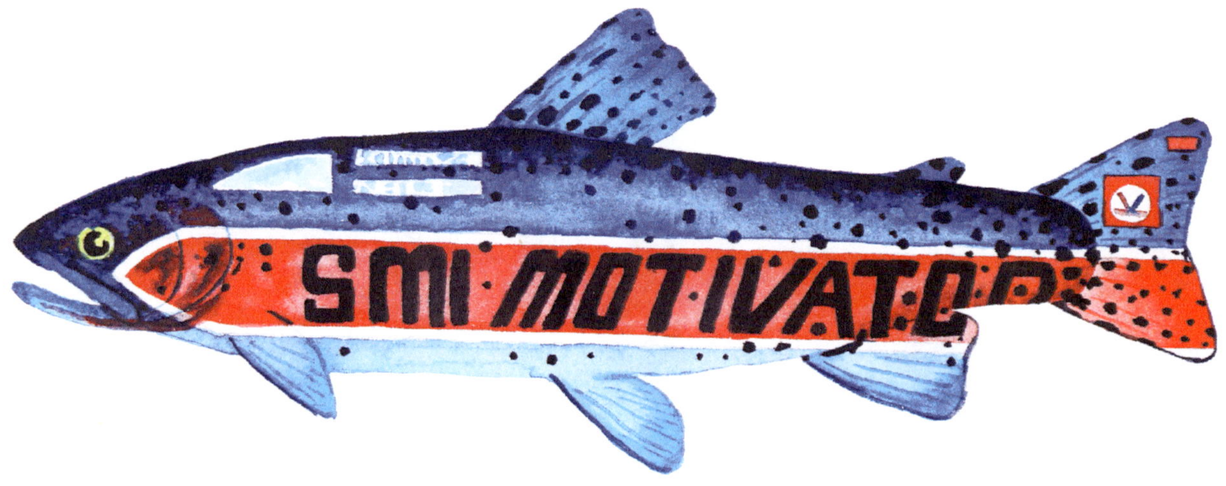

Oncorhynchus clarkii alvordensis (female)

The Alvord Cutthroat Trout, like the Alvord Desert where it lives, does not get the recognition the Bonneville Cutthroat and Bonneville Salt Flats do. This overlooked trout survives harsh conditions and as a result is a fierce fighter. At least the female Alvord Trout are tremendous fighters, the males' fighting abilities are unremarkable.

The female resembles the racecar SMI Motivator. Driving this car, Kitty O'Neil set a world speed record in 1976 on the flats of the Alvord Desert of southern Oregon. Her record of 621 mph was not broken until 2019. Ms. O'Neil faced many challenges in her life and it made her want to do more difficult feats. Besides holding the land speed record, she has records for highest free fall (180 feet), fastest speed on water (275 mph), and the water skiing speed record (104.85 mph).

To catch a male Alvord Cutthroat, it is recommended to slowly retrieve a nymph pattern. To catch the prized females, use a stimulator fly, one of those bungees you use between the fly line and the leader when trolling for Kokanees, to prevent the line snapping when they hit. Retrieve quickly, as though you don't want a fish to be able to catch it. Some fly fisherman like to fish from kayaks so they can troll extra fast. While passing up slower food, the female Alvord accepts the challenge and will attack fast moving flies. One angler is reported to have attached a hook to a Kitty O'Neil action figure and trolled it through the lake at speeds exceeding 45 mph and had great success.

https://en.wikipedia.org/wiki/Alvord_Desert
https://en.wikipedia.org/wiki/Kitty_O%27Neil
http://www.bcadventure.com/ronnewman/rainbow.phtml
http://www.nativetroutflyfishing.com/alvordcutthroat.htm

Willow-Whitehorse Creek Cutthroat Trout

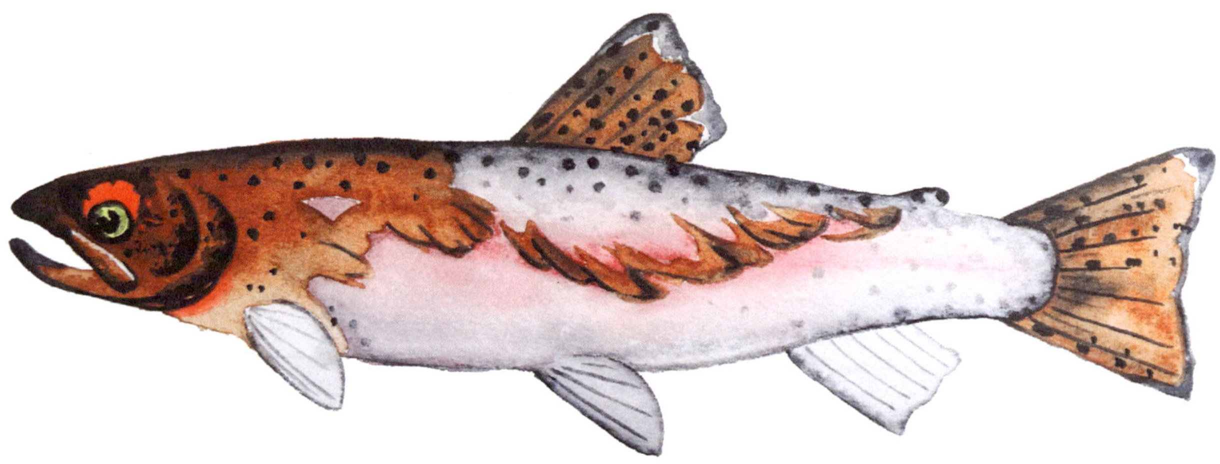

Oncorhynchus clarkii subsp.

The name of this cutthroat conjures up the frozen north: willow ptarmigan, dogsleds, the aurora borealis, and Sam McGee smiling from inside that furnace.

The Willow–Whitehorse Creek Cutthroat was a Lahontan Trout back in the Pleistocene. As the glaciers receded, Lake Lahontan shrank forming several other lakes. In these separated lakes, several different cutthroat evolved.

Like its namesake, the Willow Ptarmigan, this trout has camouflage that changes with the seasons. It is white in the summer when the blinding desert sun turns the surface of the water silvery and dark brown in the winter when the low sun creates a dark lake. The cutthroat illustrated is a male with between-seasons coloring. The male develops a red patch above its eye, like the ptarmigan, during spawning season. A pinkish hue can be seen along the lateral line, a vestige of their Lahontan ancestry.

https://www.nsf.gov/news/mmg/mmg_disp.jsp?med_id=68953

Humboldt Cutthroat Trout

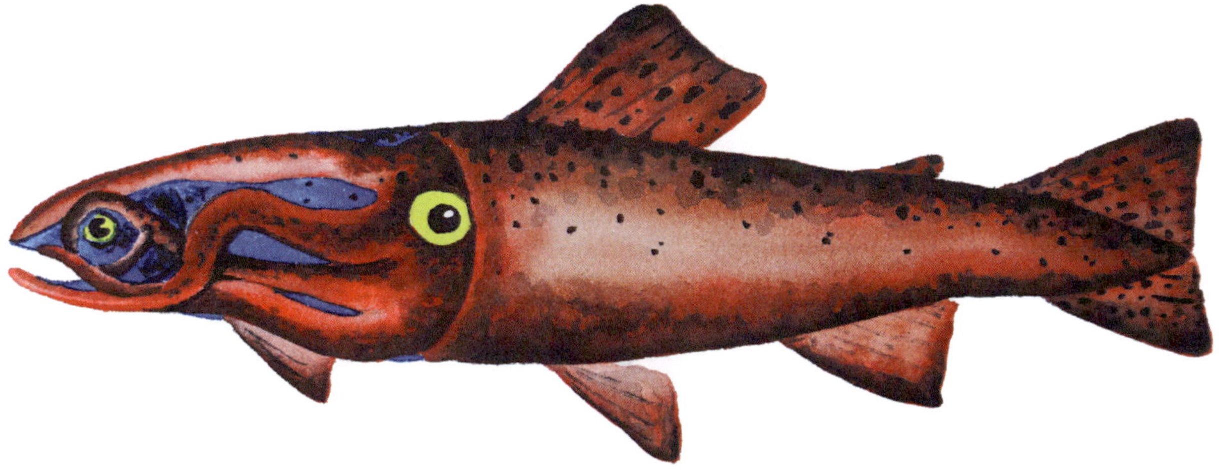

Oncorhynchus clarkii subsp.

The Humboldt Cutthroat Trout displays the first known example of animal Vavilovian Mimicry. In Vavilovian Mimicry, weeds mimic the crops they grow in so they will not be pulled or sprayed with herbicide. In the case of the Humboldt Cutthroat Trout, it took on the appearance of its main predator, the Humboldt Squid. Back in the Pleistocene when lakes, rivers, and seas all intermingled, the Humboldt Cutthroat Trout was the same size as the Humboldt Squid, about four feet long. The squid, with their squid brains, would see a Humboldt Cutthroat Trout and think, "hey look at Joe over there, he just caught a trout". Today, SCUBA divers fear the Humboldt Squid as they sometimes attack. The Humboldt Squid is also called the *Diablo Rojo* as it flashes reds and whites while hunting. It is not known if the Humboldt Cutthroat Trout does the same. This will require further fishing, oops, I mean research.

https://en.wikipedia.org/wiki/Humboldt_squid
https://en.wikipedia.org/wiki/Aggressive_mimicry#:~:text=Aggressive%20mimicry%20stands%20in%20semantic,an%20aposematic%20or%20harmful%20model.

Bear Lake Strain of the Bonneville Cutthroat Trout

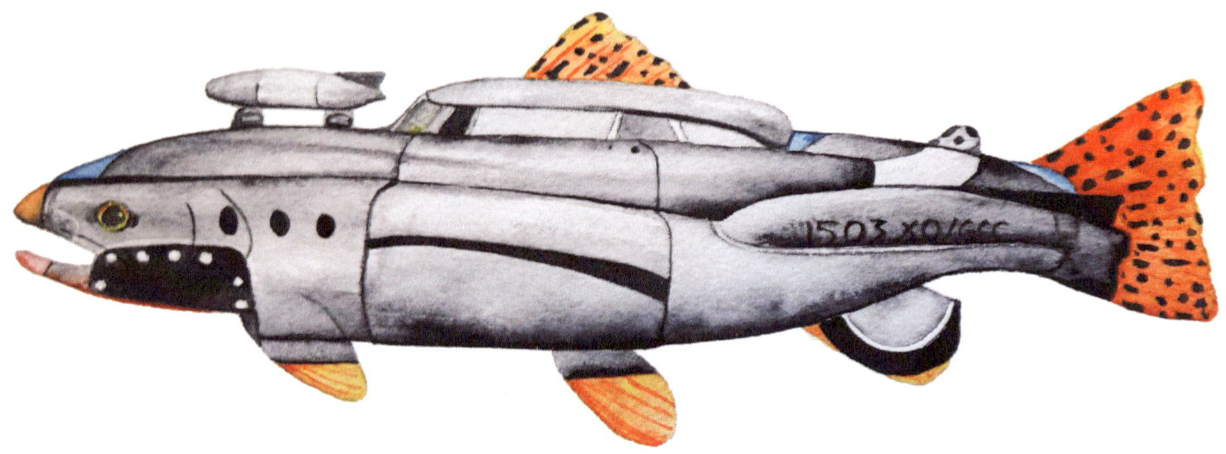

Oncorhynchus clarkii utah

Hang on when you hook into one of these robust cutthroat trout. Fisherman have clocked the Bear Lake Strain of the Cutthroat Trout at 165.735 mph.

This trout has an uncanny resemblance to a 1952 Buick Super Riviera. The sides are a beautiful brushed aluminum color lightly freckled with large Carlsbad black spots. They appear to change color depending on their surroundings and the changing light conditions.

These trout are finicky feeders. Fly tier Jeff Brock has found this trout's weakness after years of trial and error, a fly he calls Bombshell Betty. He ties them in 16 colors: Carlsbad Black, Verde Green, Imperial Blue, Barton Grey, Victoria Maroon, Seamist Grey, Sky Grey, Terrace Green, Venetian Blue, Surf Blue, Glenn Green, Sequoia Cream, Apache Coral, Golden Sand, Beach White, and Teal Blue. Mr. Brock says all are equally good depending on the conditions. They come in hook sizes of 14, 12, 10, and 8.

If my math is correct, a set of one fly of each color and size is 64 flies. You should always have at least one back up, so that brings your total to 128 flies. Even though Mr. Brock prides himself on buying his materials at thrift stores, he sells them for $5 each. This brings your total to fish for these trout to $640 for flies alone. This doesn't include gas, beer, food, and campground fee. Mr. Brock has to make a living too.

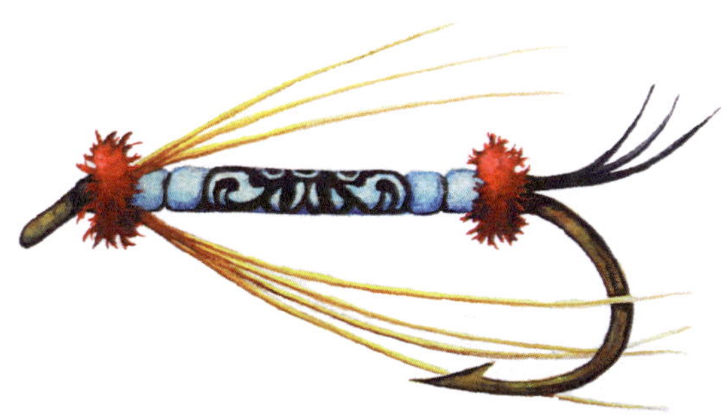

Bombshell Betty
*Thrift store materials: red cashmere sweater, Teal Blue bra
with black lace and 2mm padding, blonde wig, and black false
eyelashes*

Provo River Strain of the Bonneville Cutthroat Trout

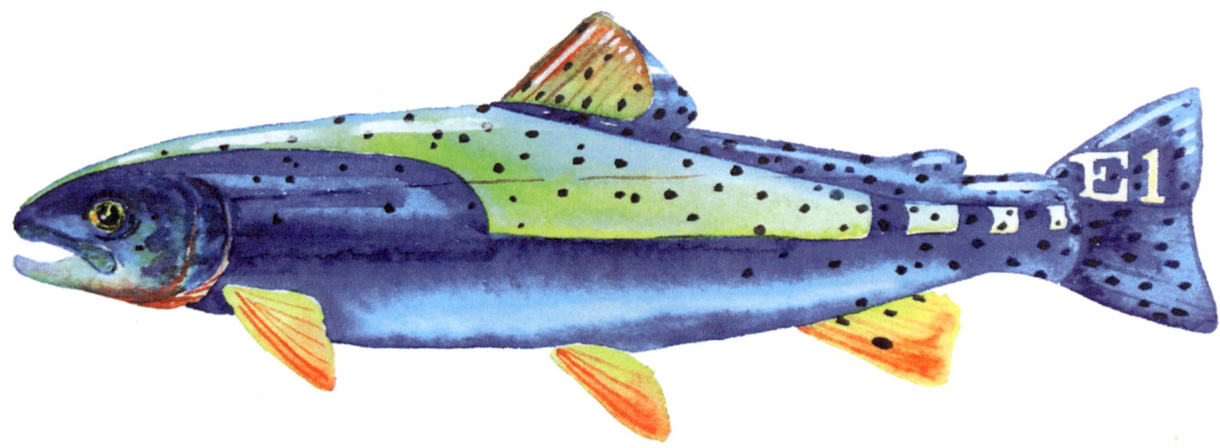

Oncorhynchus clarkii utah

This cutthroat is extremely fast, but not in the wild sense. After all, it is from the Provo River which ends up in Provo, Utah, home of Brigham Young University. Besides having speed, this cutthroat is extremely quiet, so quiet that their prey do not have a chance to escape their swift, silent attack. Their numbers are doing well as they have large, healthy wholesome families and do an incredibly good job of raising them through their first four stages of development: egg, alevin, fry, and juvenile. Once they reach adulthood they are on their own, as it should be. The E1 marking on the tail is similar to the marking on the electric race car, Electric Blue. BYU students built and raced the Electric Blue on the Bonneville Salt Flats. In 2014 it broke electric car speed records with a blistering 204.9 miles per hour.

https://en.wikipedia.org/wiki/Provo_River
https://news.byu.edu/news/byu-electric-car-breaks-200-mph-barrier-set-new-land-speed-record

Snake Valley Strain of the Bonneville Cutthroat Trout

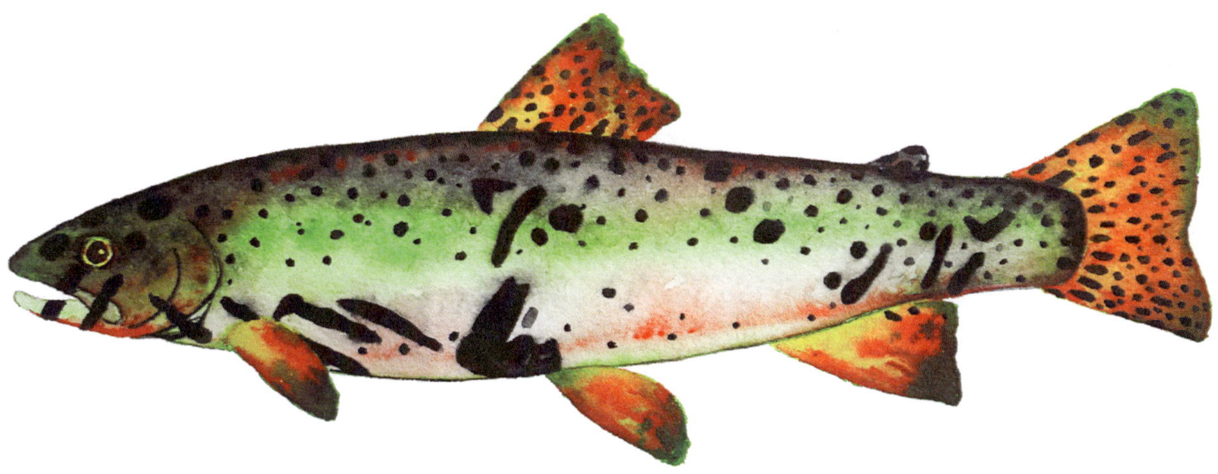

Oncorhynchus clarkii utah

The facial markings of the Snake Valley strain of the Bonneville Cutthroat Trout are often confused with the markings of several of the Snake River Fine-spotted Cutthroat Trout. Many fly fishermen, trying to complete their life list of North American trout, never complete their list because of this confusion. On seeing the snake-like head rising out of the water, many fishermen shudder involuntarily and sever the line.

We once lived a little north of Bangkok. There was a neighborhood story about giant snakes that swam in our lake and ate the family cats. I never got to see one, but my wife got to see two cobras in our neighborhood, the lucky duck.

The markings of this cutthroat are believed to be a form of camouflage that allow them to hide among reflections of the bear-clawed Aspens lining the Snake River. This keeps them safe from searching osprey, eagles, and fishermen.

Snake River Fine-Spotted Cutthroat Trout

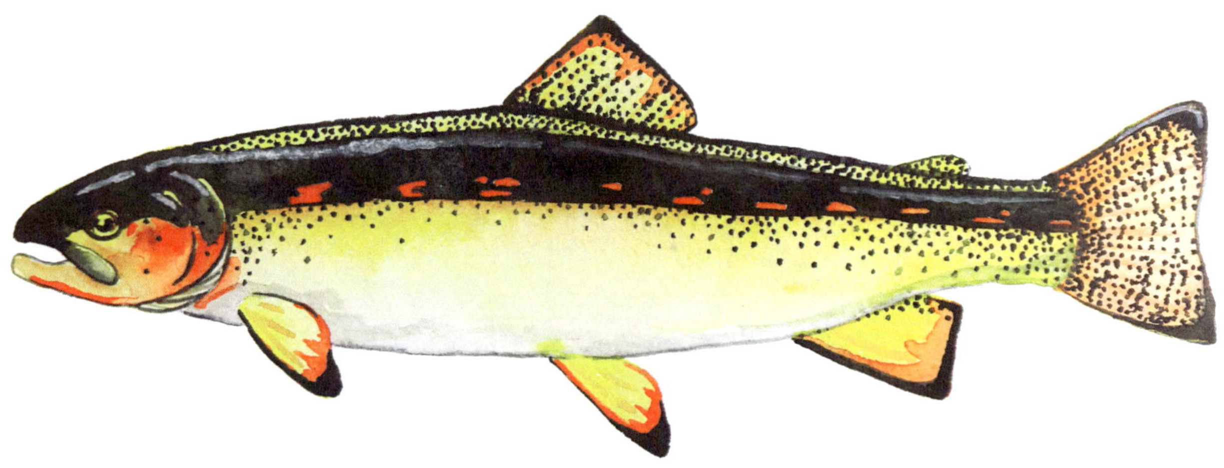

Oncorhynchus clarkii behnkei (Western Terrestrial Garter Snake variation)

Not everyone enjoys fishing for the Snake River Fine-Spotted Cutthroat Trout. Actually, it is the landing and handling that bothers some fishermen. The trout and their river are named after the many snakes that live around and in the river. Yes! They live in the river. Snakes can swim on and under the surface. When I was a kid, I caught a garter snake with a lump in in it and I just had to know what the lump was. With some gentle massaging the snake threw up a fish. Another time I saw one swimming across the surface of a pond with a pair of frog legs sticking out of its mouth. At some time in my life, I was watching a video that showed how currents worked underwater in a stream. The videographer had a camera on a stick. One of the scenes showed a rattlesnake curled up under a rock. Yikes. It gives me the heebie-geebies to think about the first backpacking trip my wife and I did together. On the last day we were rinsing off in a large pool in the stream. I stood up to look at a rock on a high bank about chest high. There was a rattlesnake staring back at me. We packed up and left and it seemed like we heard a rattler every hundred yards as we hiked the trail out. I still get the shivers thinking about all the rattlesnakes that must have been under the water.

Some Variations of the Snake River Fine-Spotted Cutthroat Trout

Batesian Mimicry is when one harmless species resembles a dangerous species. These trout look like a variety of snakes, all sporting a multitude of fine spots. Fisherman who enjoy catching this trout also like to catch Freshwater Burbot and Moray Eels.

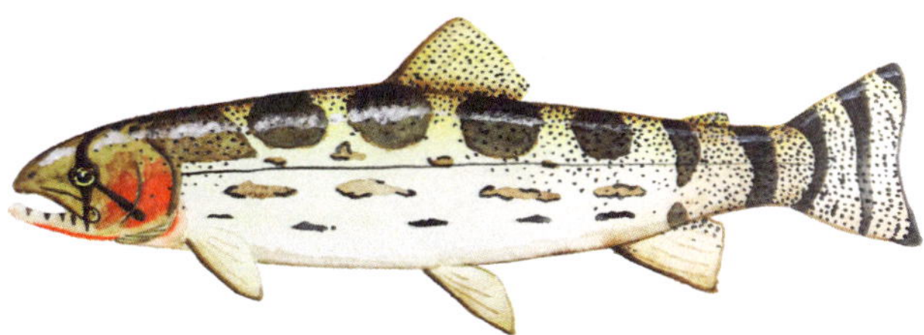

Oncorhynchus clarkii behnkei (Gopher Snake variation)

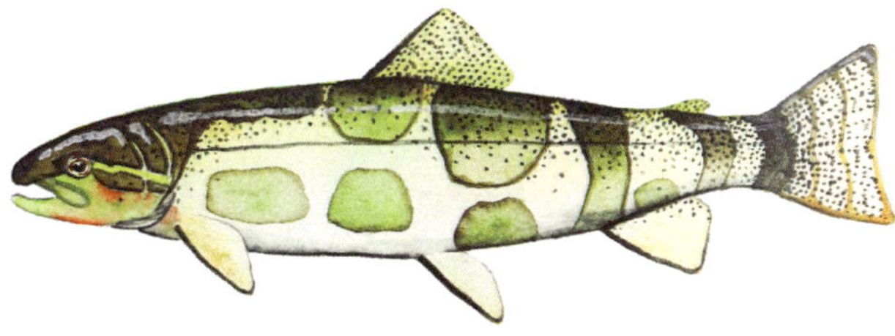

Oncorhynchus clarkii behnkei (Western Rattlesnake variation)

Yellowstone Cutthroat Trout

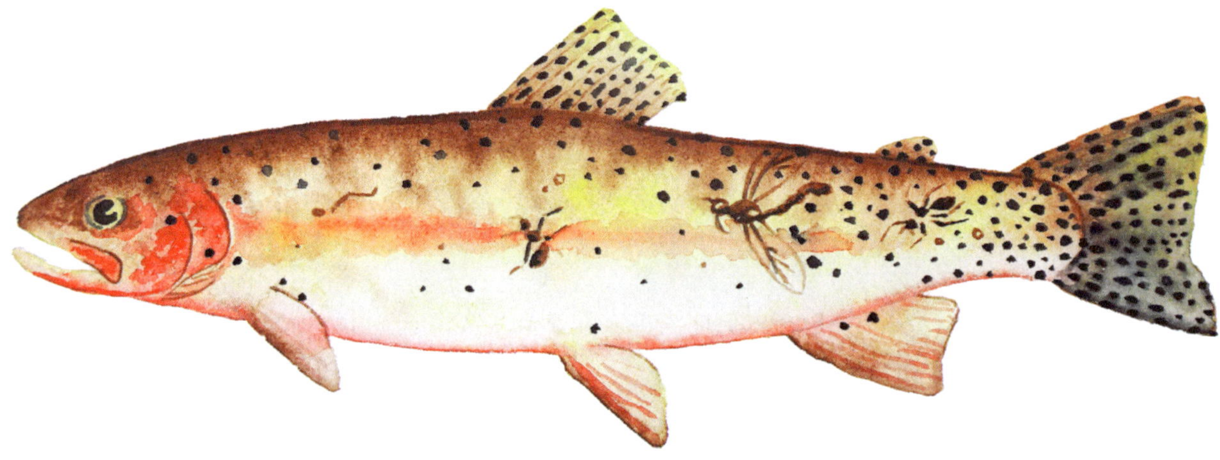

Oncorhynchus clarkii bouvieri

My wife and I have what we call Del Monte[R] moments. They are when we get the connection of a word and its origin. Our first one was Del Monte[R]. We knew the food company Del Monte[R] and we knew what del monte meant in Spanish, but never connected them together until one day it hit. They call it Del Monte[R] because the food comes from the hills. Several years ago, I was fishing the Yellowstone River and had just landed my first Yellowstone Cutthroat Trout and was admiring the tiny insects seemingly embedded in its beautiful amber sides when the Del Monte[R] moment hit me. The Yellowstone River is called this because of the yellow stones on the bottom of the river. The Yellowstone Cutthroat blends in with the amber stones of the river bottom.

In recent history, which means the last forty years to me, fly tiers have been inventing new flies left and right. Someday they are going to run out of ideas. Perhaps they can study the insects in the Yellowstone amber and start a new line of flies based on Pleistocene insects.

https://www.popsci.com/story/animals/ancient-insects-amber-colors/#:~:text=The%20insects%20can%20be%20dated,true%20color%20could%20be%20identified.

Sedge Creek or Waha Lake Cutthroat Trout

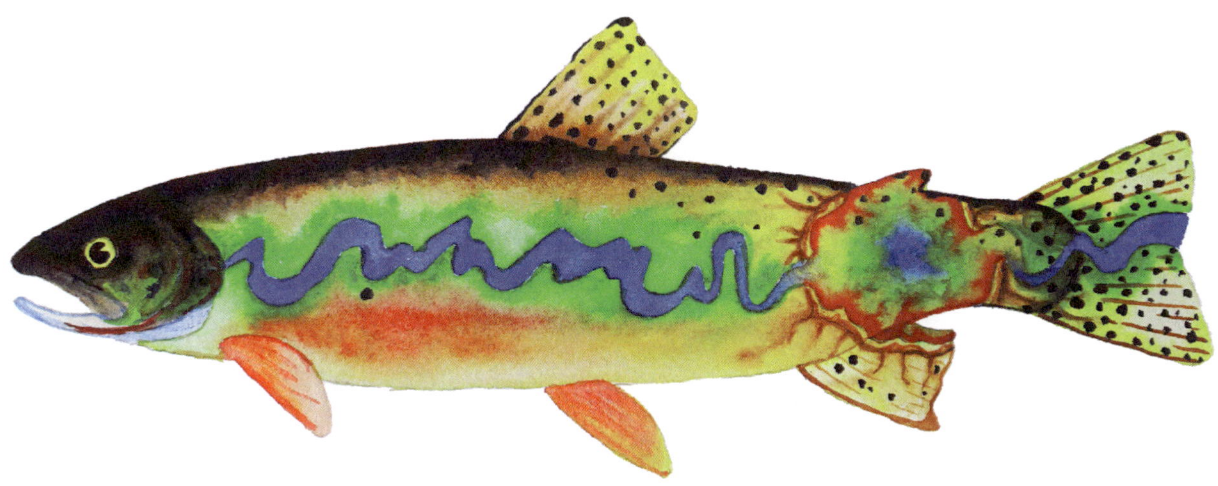

Oncorhynchus clarkii bouvieri

Shakespeare has nothing on the Sedge Creek Cutthroat Trout when it comes to diabolical plots on keeping two star-crossed lovers apart. Sedge Creek is separated from Yellowstone Lake by a steaming geothermal pool that appears to be cursed by the witches of Macbeth, "Double, double, toil and trouble; fire burn and caldron bubble". Alas, if poor Randy Rainbow was driven to hybridize with Susie Sedge Creek Cutthroat, he would be turned into trout chowder before he got halfway through the geothermal pool separating them.

https://www.americansouthwest.net/wyoming/yellowstone/pelican-valley-turbid-lake.html
https://www.poetryfoundation.org/poems/43189/song-of-the-witches-double-double-toil-and-trouble

Westslope Cutthroat Trout

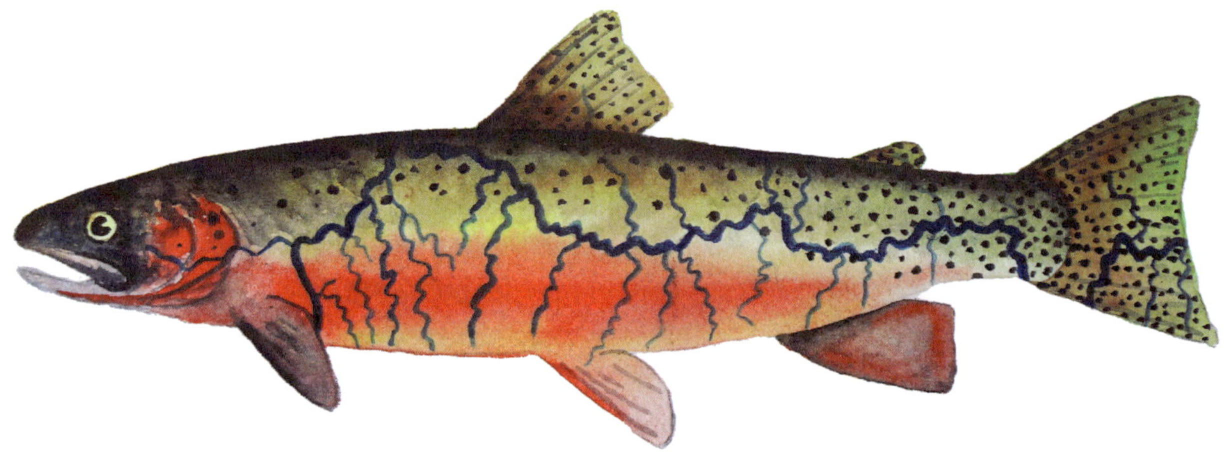

Oncorhynchus clarkii lewisi

The Westslope Cutthroat Trout has some rather unique vermiculations. Close examination reveals a map of rivers explored by Lewis and Clark. The map on this particular Westslope Cutthroat Trout is the section of the Missouri River and its tributaries that includes the great falls near modern day Great Falls, Montana.

It was below this falls where Private Silas Goodrich caught a half dozen of these trout. Captain Lewis wrote the first non-Native American description of them. The scientific name, *Oncorhynchus clarkii*, was given by John Richardson to honor Captain Clark. Later the subspecies name *lewisi* was added to honor both Captains of the Corps of Discovery. Poor Private Silas Goodrich was given no credit. In fact, Lewis and Clark were not even sure of his name, as at times they called him Goodrich, Guthrege, and Gutrich. He was recognized by Lewis as that guy who likes to fish.

I should sit down and invent a fly so I can call it the Goodrich or Guthrege or Gutrich. Perhaps, a grasshopper pattern that uses rubber legs cut from a Goodrich brand inner tube or tire.

Individual trout have different sections of Lewis and Clark's maps on their sides. They cover from St. Louis to the Pacific Ocean and back. Dedicated Westslope Cutthroat Trout fisherman are as fanatical as Pokemon collectors and they just "have to catch them all".

http://www.lewis-clark.org/article/1911

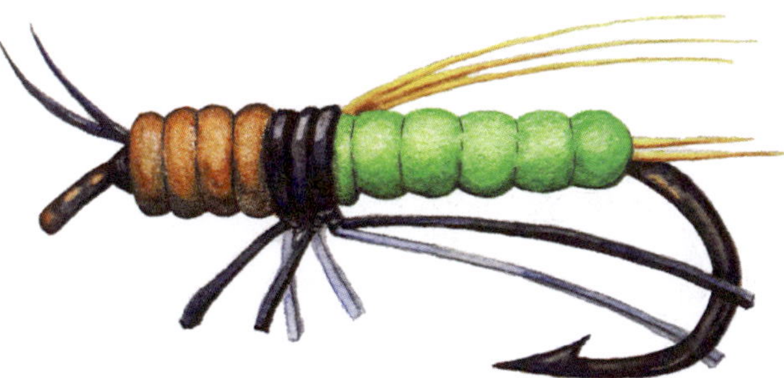

Goodrich Grasshopper
Thrift store materials: Sexy Sienna bra with 4 mm padding,
Paradise Green bra with 2 mm padding, blonde wig, black
false eyelashes, and a bicycle inner tube

Mountain Cutthroat Trout

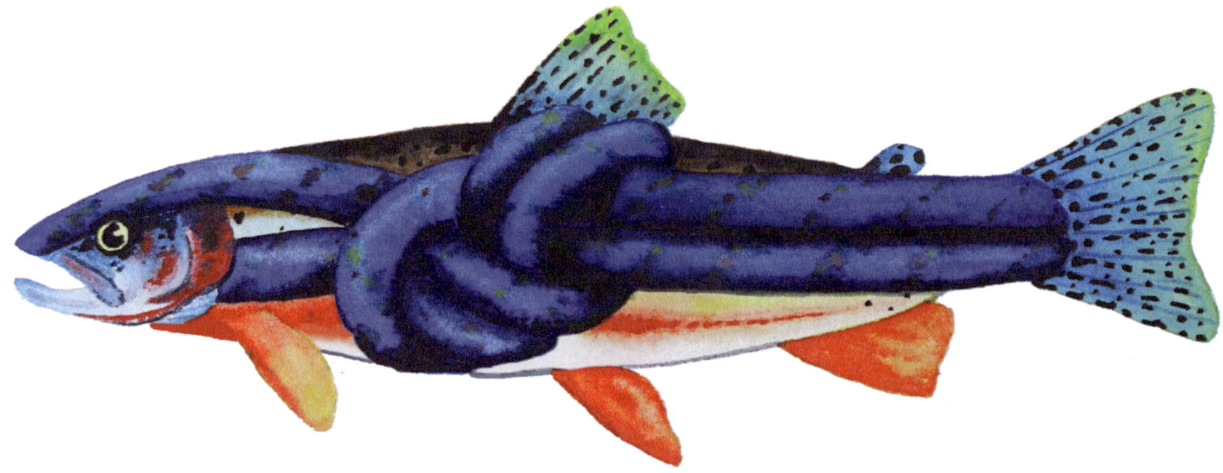

Oncorhynchus clarkii alpestris

As a young boy, my dad would take me to fish in the pool below a 100-foot waterfall. It was always exciting. To get to it, I clung to my dad's back as he leaped across parts of the stream that were too wide for me to jump across. We would fish the pool under the falls as mist soaked our clothes and the thunder of the falls vibrated our bodies with infrasound like a giant woofer at a Grateful Dead concert. I can still remember one of the trout I caught in that pool. I was messing around, like kids tend to do, and set my fly in the water with only about 6 inches of line at the end of my rod. I and the trout that immediately took that fly were equally surprised when I reacted by yanking it out of the water and onto the shore. (I still tend to overreact when setting the hook and a friend of mine laughs at me as I perform what he calls the Coulee City jerk.)

Occasionally my dad and I would take a much longer trail and look into the pools above the falls. Those pools had huge trout in them, but were off limits to fishing because a nearby town got its water from there. I always wondered how the trout got up above the falls. I was delighted to find the Mountain Cutthroat Trout in James Prosek's trout book. The lateral lines that appear to be climbing ropes and knots on their sides explain it all. They climbed up. Besides discovering how they got above the falls, it also means at some time in trout history there was an Alex Honnold of trout who free soloed up the falls while carrying ropes it could use to help others ascend. Of course, early ropes were made from natural materials found along the stream and not the modern climbing ropes that remind me of exotic snakes. Before you write me and debunk my discovery with evidence of how trout cannot weave a rope with their mouths, take a look at the recommended video of a Weaver Bird making a nest with its beak.

https://www.rei.com/learn/expert-advice/climbing-knots.html
https://films.nationalgeographic.com/free-solo
https://www.rei.com/learn/expert-advice/ropes.html
https://www.youtube.com/watch?v=BEwa_I1LK3w

Coastal Cutthroat Trout

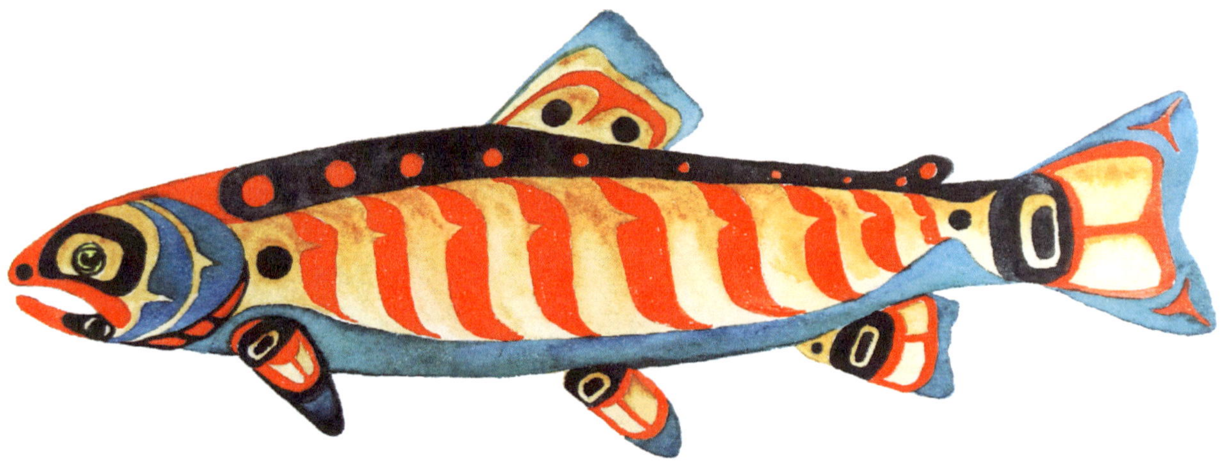

Oncorhynchus clarkii clarkii

The Coastal Cutthroat Trout resembles the artistic style created by the Native Americans of the Northwest Coast. Early Europeans arriving in this part of the world did not know what to make of the designs on this trout or the houses, poles, canoes, tools, and clothing of the Native Americans. The style was nothing like what was happening in European art circles. It was not until Picasso that it was realized how advanced this art was. In fact, Picasso should not be given such a large space in art history books and the art of the Northwest Coastal Native Americans should be expanded.

Heck, even the fish off this coast lived cubism long before Picasso and Braque were given credit for "discovering" it. The halibut starts life like a regular fish and then turns, flattening its planes and one eye migrates to the same side as the other eye.

If you fish for these trout, you may want to try these flies: 1) the *Sisiutl*, named after the double-sided serpent with a face in the middle 2) the *Yaahl Sgwansung* (The Only Raven), Bill Reid's Haida name. Bill Reid is a Haida artist who helped revitalize Northwest Coast Art or 3) the *Emily Carr*, named after one of the first white British Columbia artists to champion these people and their art.

https://en.wikipedia.org/wiki/Sisiutl
https://www.billreidgallery.ca/pages/about-bill-reid
https://en.wikipedia.org/wiki/Emily_Carr

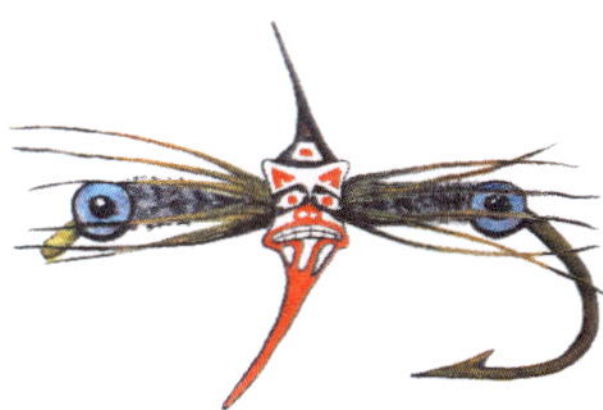

Sisiutl
*Materials: black tree lichen,
hand-painted mussel shell
eyes, hand-painted fish
vertebra, and Black-tailed
Deer hair*

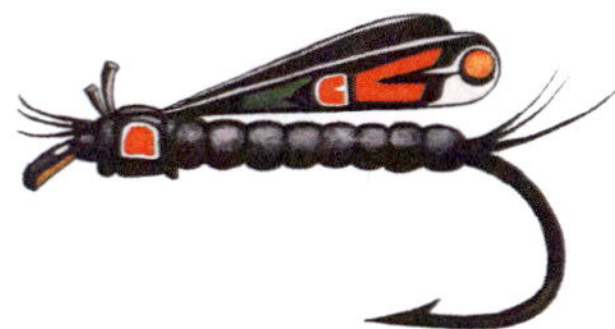

Yaahl Sqwansung
*Materials: black foam,
hand-painted feathers, and
Black-tailed Deer hair*

CHAPTER 5

BROWN TROUT AND ATLANTIC SALMON

If you follow the fish family tree back 180,000 years you will find the Brown Trout and Atlantic Salmon have a common maternal ancestor called Haplogroup B. This maternal ancestor lived in lakes of northern Europe and spawned in rivers. At the end of the last ice age, rising sea levels connected some of these lakes to the oceans. The Atlantic salmon split off at this time to form its own branch of the trout family tree.

Brown Trout

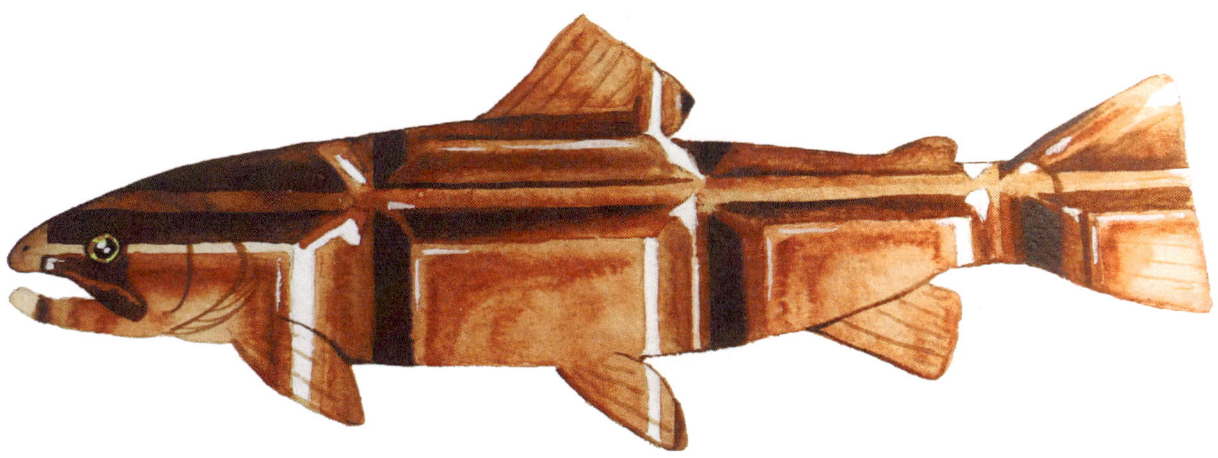

Salmo trutta fario (spawning male)

The German Brown Trout is not a native of North America. It first arrived in North America in 1883 when Fred Mather imported eggs from the president of the German Fishing Society.

The sexes of the German Brown Trout are easily told apart. The female's scales are arranged in colorful floral designs commonly found on traditional German dresses. Spawning males look like a bar of fine chocolate. Fred Mather, while courting his second wife, Adelaide Fairchild, once presented her with a bouquet of wildflowers he picked along the river and a spawning male Brown Trout wrapped in newspaper (most gifts were wrapped in newspaper in the late 1800's). Her first thought was what a huge chocolate bar! Her second, not another stinking fish! She tailed the Brown and back-handed it across his surprised face. It set the relationship back quite a while. Good thing the Browns were biting and Fred kept out of sight, fishing the river for a few weeks.

The non-spawning male Brown Trout looks like a bottle of Pilsen. I have never caught a male German Brown. They are difficult to catch with a fly and I am only a mediocre fly fisherman. I refuse to use the tried-and-true Brown Spinners made from old beer bottle caps and treble hooks. The hooks are usually crowned with fragrant chunks of Limburger (there are some beer aficionados who dispute this choice of cheese and say Pilsners deserve a lighter cheese like a young Gouda). If I ever catch a male German Brown, I feel confident that I will recognize it. My fellow Peace Corps volunteers and I, in Paraguay, downed many Pilsen Pilsners when in town to collect our *sueldos*. Our favorite bar was in the sugar town of Guarambaré. The bar was run by a Chilean woman who made the best *pororo* (popcorn) and vegetarian *empanadas del horno*. She kept the head of a Toco Toucan balanced among the liquor bottles above the bar.

https://www.americanangler.com/a-rising-trout/
https://germanfoods.org/german-food-facts/beer-cheese-pairing/
https://prabook.com/web/fred.mather/1080718

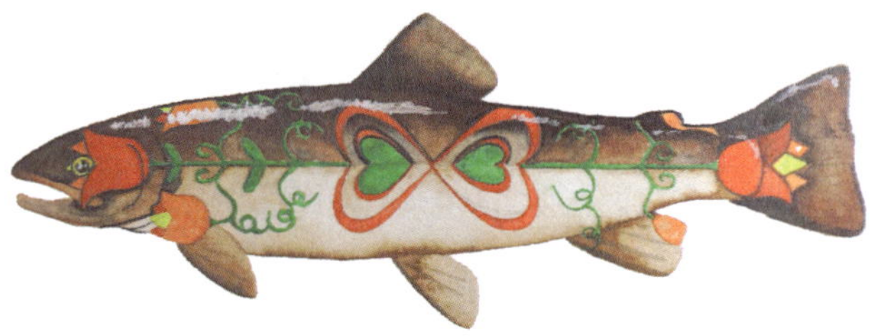

Salmo trutta fario (female)

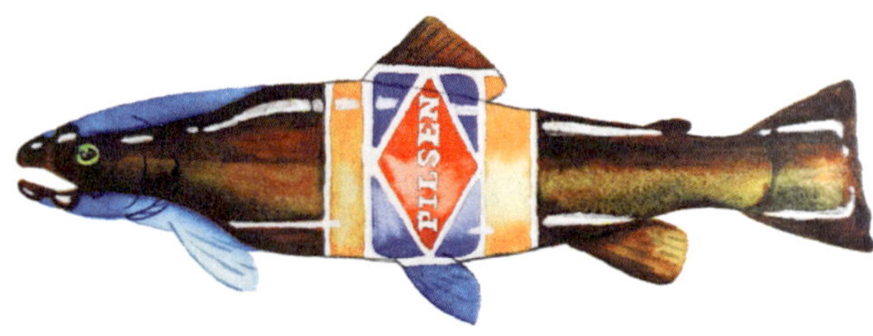

Salmo trutta fario (male)

Atlantic Salmon

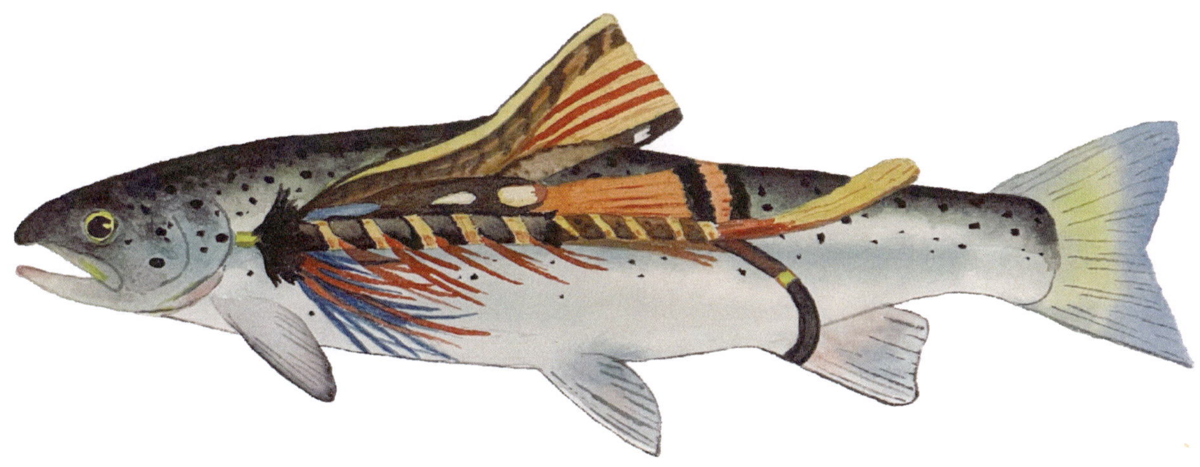

Salmo salar salar

How convenient when your prey shows you what fly to use by displaying it on its silvery flanks. Unfortunately, they change these displays almost hourly and by the time you find the correct fly to use, they are hungry for a different pattern.

The one depicted in this painting is displaying a Baron Fly designed by Mr. Farlow in the mid-19th century. Atlantic Salmon, fly fishermen, and interior decorators are attracted to Atlantic Salmon fly patterns in all of their tintinnabulatious colors. (Tintinnabulatious is a word David James Duncan uses to describe the colorful candles Steve and Satyavati make in "The River Why").

https://www.flydreamers.com/en/photo/classic-salmon-flies-pic21575

Sebago Salmon

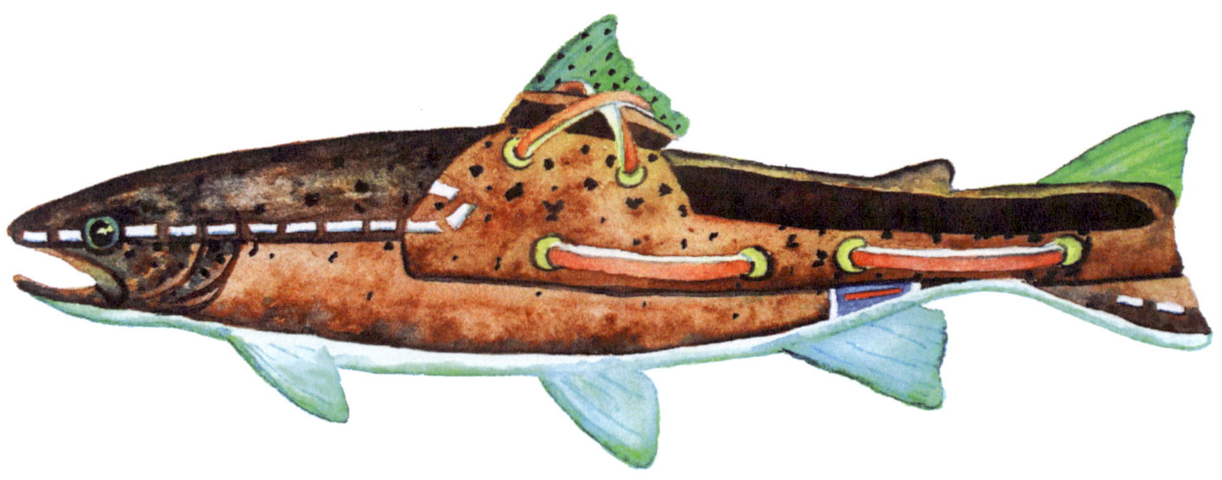

Salmo salar sebago

Like other salmon of the genus *Salmo salar*, the Sebago Salmon is quite the leaper. It performs amazing aerial stunts often followed by reel-smoking runs. Many a fisherman has had their line snapped by a runaway Sebago when burned to the end of their backing. This explains why you will often see bank fisherman scrambling up and down the slippery rocky beaches of northern New England lakes as they try to take the pressure off their straining lines. To keep from slipping, most New England Sebago Salmon fisherman wear Sebago Dockside shoes. The preferred style seems to be the Portland Waxed-Brown with a white sole. (You occasionally see a fisherman, who also likes to bowl, wearing the Portland Jibs in yellow, red, and blue.) If you have a sourie to attend after fishing, the waxed leather quickly wipes clean. I hear a Magic Erasers work wonders at cleaning the algae stains off of the white soles.

https://sebago-usa.com/

Ouananiche Salmon

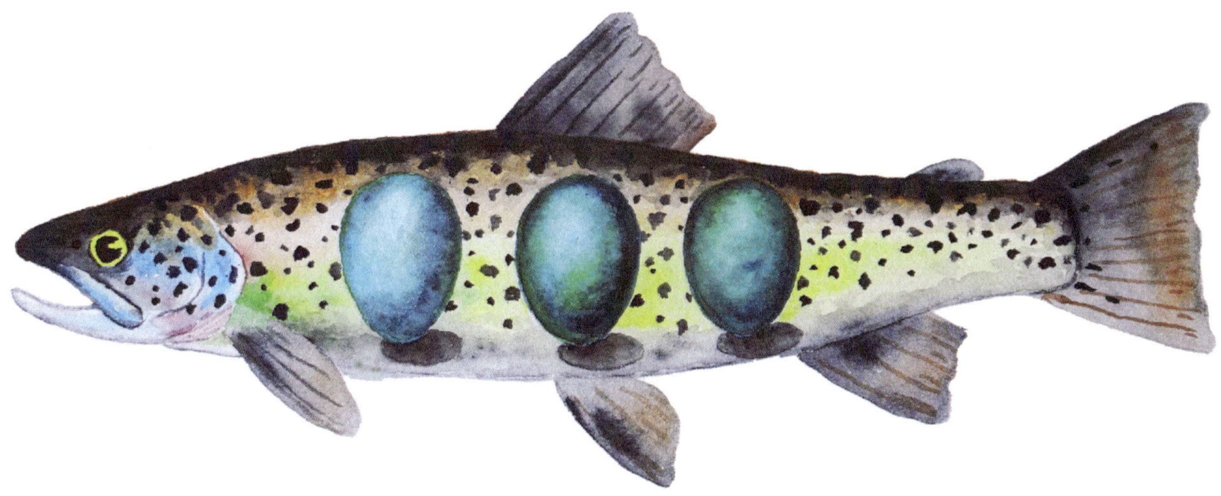

Salmo salar ouananiche

I love how the blue Araucana egg spots appear three dimensional and stand out against the yellow sides of this beautiful salmon. The name of this salmon is a combination of the Montagnais name for this salmon and quiche, a traditional way to serve this salmon (ouanans + quiche = ouananiche).

Here are the ingredients for Salmon Quiche or just Ouananiche: 1 homemade quiche crust (9" pie dish), 1 tbsp unsalted butter, 1 leek, 8 spears fresh asparagus, 2 garlic cloves (my favorite garlic is Inchelium Red from Filaree Farms), 3/4 cup grated Gruyere cheese, 5 eggs (preferably homegrown Araucana eggs), 1/4 tsp salt, 1 1/2 cups cream, 1 pinch black pepper, 7 oz smoked Ouananiche Salmon , and 1/4 tbsp fresh dill. Bake at 350 degrees Fahrenheit for 35 minutes until the edge of the crust is brown and the eggs have set.

https://en.wiktionary.org/wiki/wananish
https://en.wikipedia.org/wiki/Montagnais
https://www.recipetineats.com/salmon-quiche/

CHAPTER 6

HYBRIDS AND TRULY FICTIONAL TROUT

Hybridization is one of the major threats to many of the trout in this book. The possible combinations seem endless, each combination having some clever name like Lahobow or Gilbert's Golden Eagle Trout. Only a few have been included in this book. They are the Tiger, Triploid, and Timber Trout. These are often referred as the Big Three Double T's by trophy trout fishermen.

Tiger Trout

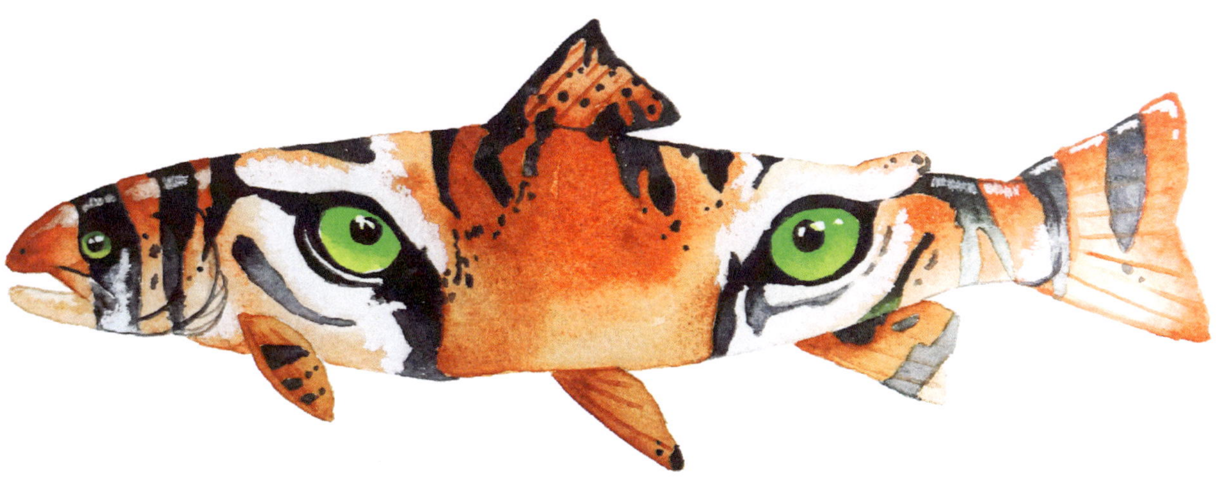

Salmo trutta x Salvelinus fontinalis (Southern variation)

The Tiger Trout is a cross between a female Brown Trout and a male Brook Trout. Most are made in a hatchery, but they can occur wherever these two species occur in nature. Two morphotypes occur. Those in the southern part of their range are orange with black stripes. Those in the northern parts of their range are white with black stripes (the one illustrated here is shown blue as it appears in the deep waters it inhabits). Many sources refer to the name of the Tiger Trout as stemming from the vermiculations on its dorsal surface and upper sides. In truth, Buss and Wright, 1958, were scientists and publicists. They knew names like Brownkie or Browk would never catch on with the fishing public or sports writers. Tiger implies a fish that is worthy of the hunt: fast, stealthy, and an incredible fighter.

Both morphotypes have eyes spots on the center of their bodies. Most fish with eyespots (Peacock Bass and Foureye Butterfly Fish are two examples) have them on the tail, so predators attack the tail instead of the head. The eye spots of the Tiger Trout are so fierce predators are stopped dead in their tracks.

Buss, K. and Wright, J.E., 1958. Appearance and fertility of trout hybrids. Trans. Am. Fish. Sot., 87: 172-181.

https://www.researchgate.net/publication/229220947_Survival_growth_and_sexual_maturation_of_the_tiger_trout_hybrid_Salmo_trutta_Salvelinus_fontinalis
https://nas.er.usgs.gov/queries/factsheet.aspx?SpeciesID=933

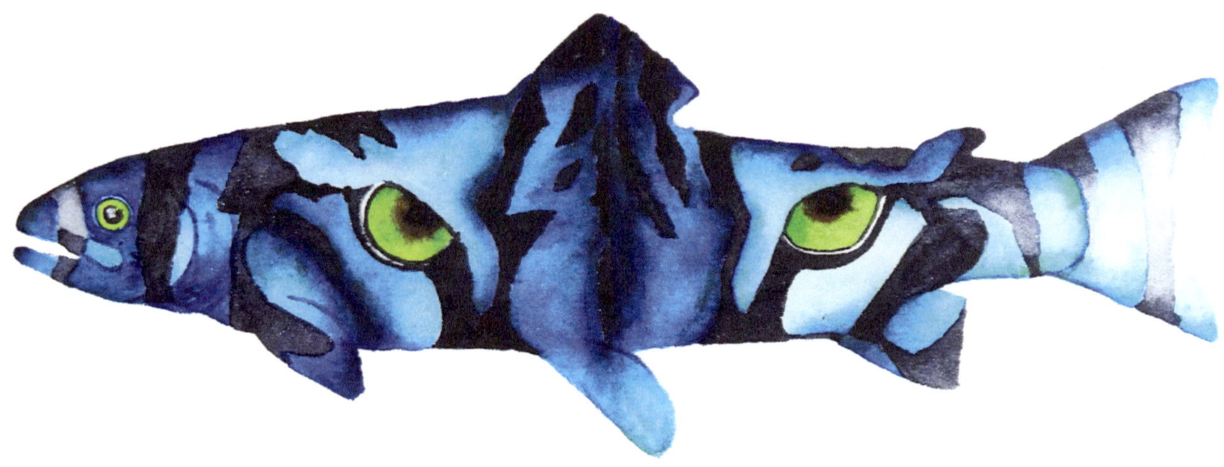

Salmo trutta x Salvelinus fontinalis (Northern variation)

Triploid Trout

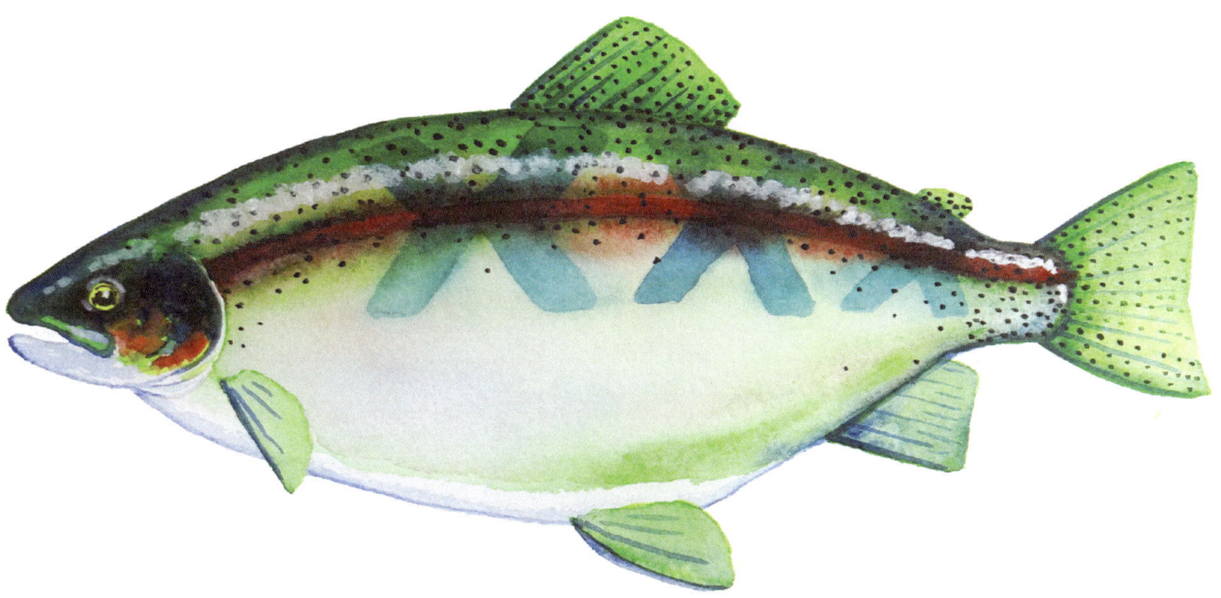

Oncorhynchus mykiss XXX

"It's not nice to fool Mother Nature" was a line from an old TV advertisement for Chiffon Soft Stick Margarine[R]. Well, this Rainbow has been fooled with. With enough fiddling and a magical chant or two it is possible to make all female Rainbows with an extra x chromosome. These trout do not reproduce, so all their energy goes into rapid growth. Another nice effect is that they cannot reproduce with native trout.

The first triploids I ever caught were in the Columbia River below pens for farmed raised trout. Not only did they grow fast, they grow extra fat and round due to the free food. They taste great on the barbeque with all of that extra fat. As their heads and tails cannot get too fat, they rather resemble a football. The fish throwing vendors at the Pike Street Market really like to throw these fish. Their shape makes for great spiral passes and Hail Mary's. One day I witnessed a Hail Mary that sailed over the bronze pig, across the street, and to the end of the line at Beecher's Cheese Shop. The receiver, in full foul-weather gear, made an amazing one-handed catch.

With a little more fiddling, colors can be manipulated and they end up looking like footballs from your favorite sports teams. As I write this, it is appropriate that my example for team colored football trout is the color of the Tampa Bay Buccaneers, the Super Bowl LV champions. Truth be told, when I painted it a couple of years ago I was thinking of the colors of the school I taught at, Okanogan High School. Perhaps state game departments can attract more fishermen and increase revenues by freeze branding team logos on these trout.

I hardly ever watch football even though I like the game. Crisp and brilliant autumn days are so precious you have to spend them wisely. Mine are usually spent out in the fields and streams. Later in the fall, when it starts to turn gloomy, I enjoy listening to a football game on the radio as I work in my shop.

https://www.youtube.com/watch?v=ijVijP-CDVI
http://www.adfg.alaska.gov/index.cfm?adfg=fishinggeneconservationlab.triploid_trout

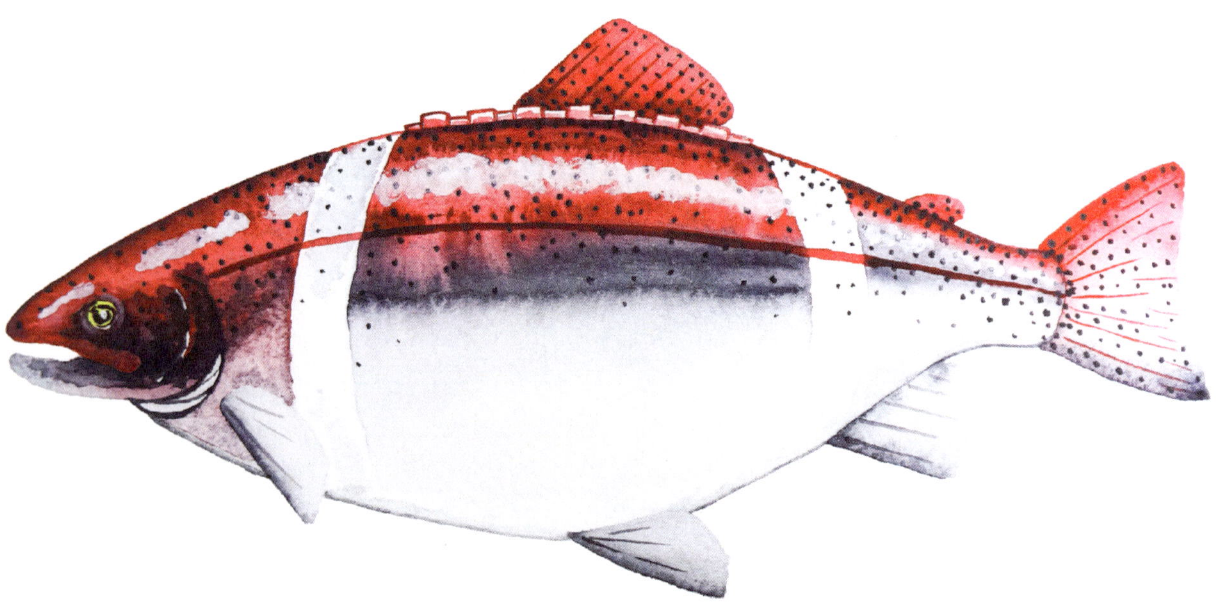

Oncorhynchus mykiss XXX (Okanogan High School variation)

Timber Trout

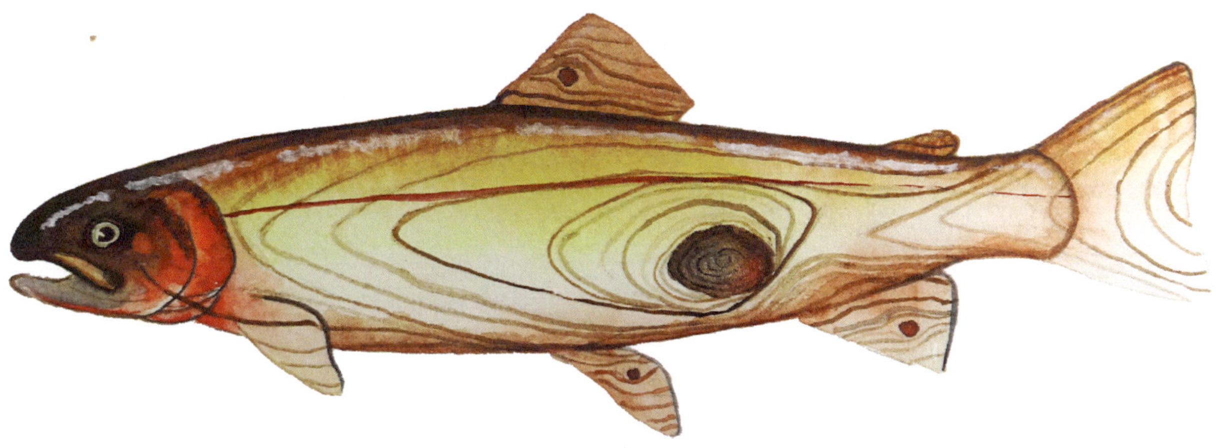

Oncorhynchus mykiss pinus ponderosa

Seems like I tend to catch more Timber Trout on days when the other trout are refusing to hit. I try everything: slower retrieves, deeper retrieves, and casts to trickier areas. Invariably, I get a strike. The light strikes are followed by action at the end of my line and my hope soars until I see the stick pulsing fish-like at the end of my line. The larger Timber Trout hit with great force and end up breaking my line.

The number of subspecies of Timber Trout are equal to the number of shrubs and trees that grow along our streams, rivers, and lakes. Actually, the number is larger as occasionally you will catch an exotic subspecies from an old pallet, teak deck chair, sunken sailboat, inlaid parcheesi game... There is a high degree of variation within a subspecies, but genetic tests have proven they are all the same subspecies. You can catch one with bark on or off, in various stages of decay, varnished or painted.

I always intend to come back and snorkel for all my lost fishing flies and lures when I am not fishing, hunting, gardening, sleeping, backpacking, skiing, painting, sculpting, teaching, and when conditions are better. I rarely do, so if you would like some poorly tied flies, I can tell you where to snorkel. My wife and I snorkel our local river once a summer. It is great fun to watch fish, freshwater mussels, and colorful river rock as we glide by.

Acknowledgements

I lucked out in finding someone to share my life with. You think you know someone when you marry, but the years have proved I am pretty darn lucky that Susan accepted me. She keeps me active and we have had and continue to have some amazing adventures together.

Elliot, Jaime, and Svea are incredible people despite it being my first try at being a father, father-in-law, and exchange student host parent. I love having them in my life.

My parents introduced me to the natural world. My mom never complained about all the creatures I brought into the house. My dad taught me to fish and is still a fishing partner. Thank you for everything Mom and Dad.

Glenn taught me to fly fish and was my fishing partner through college. His girlfriend, now wife, Nancy never seemed to mind that I was the third wheel on many fishing trips.

My art journey really started when Dr. Richard Johnson had me illustrate his "Key to the Mammals of Washington" when I was one of his students at Washington State University. Emily Silver's scientific illustration class and her watercolors greatly influenced my art.

My principal, Bob Shacklett, encouraged me to be the best art teacher possible while I taught at Okanogan High School.

The Confluence Gallery in Twisp, Washington first started showing my work many years ago when I still had much to learn. Sybil, the gallery director, seemed to know the direction to point me in. Virginia Sterling bought some of my early work and invited Susan and I into her home. She was instrumental in my decision to sculpt.

Richard Beyer shared his humor and experience with me. All of the artists at the Confluence gallery continually teach me what it is to be an artist. I am lucky I can call many of them friends.

Gary Headlee, keeps me thinking artistically with his almost daily texts about some cool art he is making or has seen.

Again, thank you to James Proseck.

All of my students throughout the years have taught me there is value in everyone and we all have a place in this world. Many of my students outshine me as artists and I appreciate they still learned a little from me.

Recommended Reading and Listening

Most of these titles will not improve your trout knowledge or make you a better fisherman. I enjoy them all for various reasons and think you may too.

Beyer, Margaret W. *The Art People Love*. Pullman: Washington State University Press, 1999.
Duncan, David James. *The River Why*. Toronto: Bantam Books, 1984.
Larson, Gary. *The Complete Far Side*. Kansas City: Andrews McNeel, 2014.
Proseck, James. *Trout: An Illustrated History*. New York: Alfred A. Knopf, 1996.
Ruark, Robert. *The Old Man and The Boy*. New York: Henry Holt and Co., 1957.
Service, Robert. *The Spell of the Yukon*. New York: Dodd, Mead, and Co., 1907.
Zern, Ed. *To Hell with Fishing*. New York: Appleton-Century Crofts, Inc., 1945.

Steve Forbet. *Jackrabbit Slim*. Nemperor. 1979.
Danbert Nobacon & the Axis of Dissent. *Stardust to Darwinstuff*. Verbal Burlesque Records. 2017.
Shorty and Slim. *Life on Mango Street*. CD Baby. 2008.
Ray Troll and the Ratfish Wranglers. *Where the Fins Meet the Frets*. Ray Troll and the Ratfish Wranglers. 2008.
Rick Vito. *Mojo on My Side*. Delta Groove Music. 2015.

Originals and Prints

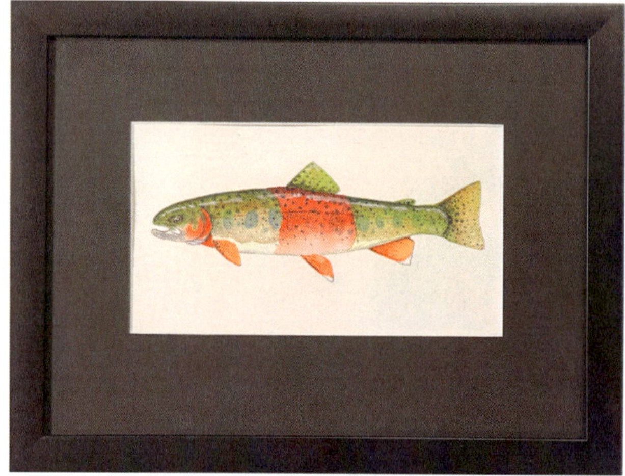

The original watercolors used to make this book can be purchased by contacting me at danbrown@danbrownart-work.com. The frames are 12" x 16". The wood frame is 1" wide and 1.5" deep. The mat opening may vary in size depending on the species of trout. When you contact me, I will let you know what trout species are still available. I will sign the original while framing it for you. The price is $800 plus tax and shipping. If you do not hear from me right away, please be patient, I am probably off fishing somewhere without Wifi or cell phone reception.

Prints, coffee mugs and more are available at www.zazzle.com/store/danbrownartwork. The collections are organized similar to the chapters in this book.

www.ingramcontent.com/pod-product-compliance
Lightning Source LLC
Chambersburg PA
CBRC090745110726
48005CB00008B/976